Midlothian Mayhem

Midlothian Mayhem

Murder, Miners and the Military in old Midlothian

Malcolm Archibald

Copyright (C) 2020 Malcolm Archibald
Layout design and Copyright (C) 2020 by Next Chapter
Published 2020 by Reality Plus – A Next Chapter Imprint
Edited by Marilyn Wagner
Cover art by Cover Mint
All rights reserved. No part of this book may be reproduced or transmitted in any form or by any means, electronic or mechanical, including photocopying, recording, or by any information storage and retrieval system, without the author's permission.

For Cathy

Contents

	INTRODUCTION	1
1	HISTORICAL AND GEOGRAPHICAL BACKGROUND	3
2	THE COLLIERS: FIGHTING FOR FREEDOM	20
3	FIGHTING FOR IMPROVEMENT	31
4	THE KILLING AT THE COAL PIT	47
5	EARLY POLICING IN MIDLOTHIAN	57
6	THE NAVVIES	73
7	RESURRECTION MEN	86
8	THE PENTLAND STILLS	93
9	THE MILITARY IN MIDLOTHIAN	105
10	DANGEROUS DALKEITH	120
11	KEEP IT IN THE FAMILY	133
12	ROBBERY IN DALKEITH	146

13	SURVIVING THE HIGHWAYS	156
14	THE SILVERBURN MURDER	177
15	THE LAST HANGING	181
16	WHO WERE THE DUELLISTS?	190
17	THE POACHERS	195
18	TROUBLE AT VOGRIE	205
19	PERILOUS PENICUIK	209
EPILOGUE		212
ABOUT THE AUTHOR		214
SELECTED BIBLIOGRAPHY		215

INTRODUCTION

Many of my ancestors were Midlothian miners. With names such as Flockhart, Junar and Hood, they toiled under the ground and lived in Gowkshill, Cockpen and Stobshill. Others were Midlothian ploughmen, working some of the most productive soil in Scotland, with the serrated ridge of the Pentlands as a backdrop and the snell wind biting at them from every quarter. One or two were soldiers, hefting their rifles as they faced the enemy of crown and country. They left few memorials to their lives but to judge by census and other records, they were decent, hardworking, honest folk and nobody can ask more than that.

Squeezed between the capital city of Edinburgh and the Scottish Borders, the county of Midlothian has a fascinating history that includes medieval battles, Covenanters, industrial disputes, fertile farms, powerful landowners, a strong military presence, tragedy and crime. This eclectic little book will concentrate on aspects of Midlothian history in the eighteenth and nineteenth centuries, a period when the county and the entire country, changed dramatically. Industrialisation spread, ideas of political reform took root and Britain emerged from a series of bruising wars with France to find herself the leading maritime power in the world. During this era, particularly in the early nineteenth century, the powers-that-be fretted over what they viewed as a tidal wave of political unrest and crime that threatened to upset the established order that kept them at the top.

Were these years so terrible or were the elite only magnifying some minor unrest for their own purposes? It is possible that there was unrest from the so-called "lower orders," but was this period a terrifying era for crimes? Were people afraid to leave their beds in case wild men and women attacked them? Were houses always prone to robbery and travellers liable to attack?

Perhaps not, but Midlothian certainly had its share of strife, social upheaval and crime.

This small book will look at some of the groups of people who were significant in Midlothian during this period, the police and the military, who ultimately defended the established order, and the colliers, who sought a better life. It will also look at some of the crimes that affected ordinary people. As an area that included both industrial and rural lives, Midlothian could be seen as a microcosm of Scotland. It had great triumphs and something of the dark side, murder and brutal assaults, drunken squabbles and riots, poisoning and highway robbery, theft and betrayal. In the past, some people have asked me why the nineteenth-century witnessed such an interest in crime. The answer could be because that century saw the beginning of a professional police force, the alteration from a rural to an urban economy and from horse to machine power.

This book is not in any way an academic examination of Midlothian, but an introduction to some aspects of the county, nothing more. Hopefully, the reader will find this look at some of Midlothian's past as fascinating as I did myself. And my ancestors, who lived through it, probably knew some of the people involved.

Malcolm Archibald

Chapter 1

HISTORICAL AND GEOGRAPHICAL BACKGROUND

At one time it was also known as Edinburghshire, the area of fertile, rolling farmland, moors and low hills immediately to the south of the Scottish capital city. On the west it is bounded by the friendly green hills of the Pentlands; on the east, it slides serenely into the fertile plain of East Lothian while, to the south, the bleak Moorfoot Hills and the windy heights of Soutra act as a partial barrier to the frontier lands of the Scottish Borders. In the eighteenth and nineteenth century, it was larger, encompassing what is today the southern suburbs of Edinburgh, spreading south to the Borders and wrapping around to the west, to where Corstorphine and Cramond now lie snug within the precincts of the capital.

Now, Edinburghshire is known as Midlothian, one of the most intriguing areas of Scotland, which itself is a land of surreal beauty, myth, legend and a few millions of the most dynamic people on the planet. Midlothian boasts a history that stretches as far back as human settlement. From at least the times of the Romans, armies have marched this way. As the epic poem, *The Gododdin* proclaims, the sixth century king Mynyddog of Gododdin sent his three hundred warriors south from Din Eidyn- Edinburgh - to challenge the invading Angles. The enemy launched the inevitable counterstroke, and the Angle-Saxons occupied the Lothians for centuries until the Scots marched south to claim the territory. Sir William Wallace, Guardian of Scotland, was said to be here, and in the fourteenth century, the Scottish resistance fighters known as the Grey Wolves made their home in the Pentland hills as they harried and harassed English invaders. Covenanters fought and worshipped in the green cleuchs of the Pentlands, stagecoaches rattled over the roads, and the industrial revolution brought the railways and the men who made them. There was mining, milling and paper-making, the gradual growth of settlements into small towns and the slow, steady pace of the farming season. Naturally, all these events left their mark, and this little corner of Scotland has archaeological sites from the Iron Age, castles and chapels from the Middle Ages, mansion houses from the eighteenth century and an industrial heritage second to none.

Naturally, such a fertile area attracted the attention of invaders, and bloody battles were fought in Midlothian, notably Roslin, Crichton and Rullion Green.

The battle of Roslin is less known now than it once was, but the story, if not historical fact, speaks of the Scots defeating the English three times in one day. Perhaps the battle is less famous than other Scottish victories because the victor was John Comyn, Bruce's rival for the throne, rather than the more acceptable Wallace or Bruce. Legend provides colourful, if doubtful, details and claims that eight thousand Scots faced near four times that many English. Confident of their numbers, the English split into three separate divisions, and the Scots defeated them one by one. Legend also speaks of thirty-five thousand casualties and bodies choking the nearby burn. Romance says that the battle occurred because Lady Margaret of Dalhousie rejected the advances of the English commander of Edinburgh Castle and married Lord Sinclair of Roslin instead.

Geoffrey Barrow, in his book *Robert Bruce*, provides a more sober appraisal of the battle, with Comyn and Simon Fraser leading a Scottish force that defeated the leading division of an English army. A second English division rescued some of the prisoners and both sides recoiled. It was not quite a major victory, but certainly a battle worth recording while place-name evidence, with Killburn and Shinbane Field, tend to prove the reality of the combat, if not the details.

If history has dimmed the Battle of Roslin, it has all but forgotten the encounter at Crichton, which took place outside Crichton Castle in 1337 during the Second War of Independence. Sir Andrew Murray was besieging the English garrison of Edinburgh Castle when an English relieving force moved north from Carlisle. Murray met them at Crichton, sent them back south again and that is just about all that is known of that encounter.

There is much more information about the battle of Rullion, or Rullion Green, which was fought a few miles from Penicuik on a dreich November day in 1666. At a time of religious strife, King Charles II foisted bishops and other elements of the Episcopalian Church onto the Kirk of Scotland. Many Presbyterians objected, particularly in the west of Scotland, leading to the king and government repressing these objectors, known as Covenanters, with harsh measures including fines and even execution. The Covenanters were forced to hold secret church meetings in the moors and hills, known as Conventicles, and eventually the repression became too much.

In November 1666 around 3000 poorly armed Covenanters marched to Edinburgh, naively intending to put their case before the king or his representative. Instead, the Lord Provost slammed shut the city gates and ordered out the City Guard. General Tam Dalyell, a veteran of the civil wars of the 1640s and of warfare in Russia, led the King's Scottish army to put down the Covenanters' rising. With their numbers reduced to around a thousand men, the Covenanters faced Dalyell on the slopes of the Pentlands. Inevitably, the trained soldiers won, with those Covenanters who were captured, either executed or transported. While Scotland remembers the later persecution of the Stuart supporters in the wake of the Jacobite risings, the Stuart king's repression of the Presbyterians is often forgotten.

Midlothian Mayhem

Augmenting the battles, Midlothian's history includes the Knights Templar at Roslin and at Temple. The Gaelic name of Temple was Balantradoch, meaning Town of the Warriors, which is an eminently suitable title for these formidable knights who owned the lands here. Nearby is the double-towered Borthwick Castle, where the romantic Mary, Queen of Scots once slipped over the castle wall, disguised as a page-boy, as she followed her tragic doom. Cromwell attacked the castle during his invasion of Scotland, while during Hitler's War, various national treasures were stored here. Today Borthwick is a luxury hotel.

There is scarcely a corner of Midlothian that was not the scene of some historical drama.

All through the Middle Ages, Scotland lived with the threat of English invasion and Midlothian, without natural defences to the south, was one of the most vulnerable areas. In 1455, the parliament passed an act that provided for early warning of invasion, with signal fires by night and smoke by day. A single bale on fire was a warning that the English were coming. Two bales meant that they are coming fast, and four indicated that the enemy was in great force. These bale fires were situated from the Border all the way north, with a beacon on Soutra Edge the focal point for Lothian attention.

These warning fires would cause a scurry of activity as men and women either grabbed their spears and prepared to defend their land or ran for shelter in the hills. Meanwhile, the great lords would clang shut the portcullis of the castle gates, whistle up their manpower and prepare to fight. In the Middle Ages, castles both defended the land against invaders and served as a reminder to sometimes unruly locals that behind these massive stone walls were the lords and masters of creation: mailed knights with long swords and short sympathy for any agitating peasants. Midlothian's castles are as dramatic as any in Scotland. Borthwick with its twin towers sits by the Gore Water, guarding the route south to Galashiels. Crichton, elevated beside the Tyne, has a distinctive Renaissance diamond-patterned interior wall and its very own ghost. Roslin looms tall beside a deep gorge, with a spectacular entrance over a narrow bridge. There is also the much-altered Dalhousie Castle, visited by Edward Longshanks of England and which held out against the forces of King Henry IV of England in 1400. All these castles nailed down the land with uncompromising, enduring solidity. Today they may appear romantic; in their heyday, they were military structures, built to dominate and intimidate. Augmenting the military architecture was that of religion.

Midlothian's religious buildings may lack the scale of the Border abbeys, but none of the interest. The hollow church at Temple was once home to the Knights Templar. Better known is the more sophisticated Roslin Chapel, a short hop to the northward. William Sinclair, the builder of Roslin Chapel, "caused artificiers to be brought from other regions and forraigne kingdoms" to create this masterpiece, with its mysterious carvings and haunted atmosphere. The Welsh traveller, Thomas Pennant, visited Roslin in 1772 and termed it "a curious piece of Gothic architecture" with a "variety of ludicrous sculpture". On the other hand, the very perceptive Dorothy Wordsworth thought it "a most elegant building," with architecture that was "exquisitely beautiful". Among the most interesting symbols is a carving of maize, a plant native to North America, in a building that was erected half a century before Christopher Columbus allegedly discovered that New World.

The solitary building of Soutra Aisle, which stands on the site of a once prestigious hospital at the head of bleak Soutra Hill, is much less pretentious. Situated on the B6368, it deserves to be better known, for archaeologists have discovered a wealth of medical treasures including hemlock, opium poppy and East African cloves. Soutra was once the highest monastic site in Britain - where weary or beleaguered wayfarers could stop to rest and recuperate from what would inevitably be a fatiguing journey. A mediaeval tract gives a flavour of the times when it speaks of putting a patient to sleep with a herbal recipe dissolved in a draught of wine and "thanne men may safly kerven him" – then men may safely carve him. What a splendid piece of writing by that monk-scribe.

The aisle later served as the burial vault for the Pringles of Soutra, a use that may explain why it has survived when all visible traces of the other mediaeval buildings have disappeared.

The place names themselves hint at the layers of history, with Roman Camp Hill above Newtongrange suggesting ancient occupation, Penicuik being the Brythonic – the language of Mynyddog of Gododdin- for Hill of the Cuckoo and Gowkshill meaning the same thing in Scots. Other names also reflect the local wildlife, with Hare Moss and Ravensneuk south of Penicuik, while Bonnyrigg was a beautiful ridge and Shinbanes and the Kill Burn tell evocatively where Scots warriors defeated the invading army at Roslin and Brothershiels hints at shielings or summer pasturing. The Castlelaw souterrain tells its own story: the souterrain is within the ramparts of an Iron Age fort. A study of place names will remove the veil from much of old Midlothian to reveal a hidden, vibrant history.

Crossing the county are the highways and byways, the arteries along which trade passed, people walked or rode; stage-coaches rattled and invading armies marched. They were also hunting grounds for footpads and highwaymen, as later chapters will reveal. Until the nineteenth-century Scottish roads were notoriously poor; muddy, flooded or blocked by snow in winter, rutted and dusty in summer. The weather was hugely important in the past, influencing crops and travel as well the economy. When a storm hit Midlothian in October 1832, the Water of Leith rose ten feet (about three metres) above its normal levels. The rushing waters damaged the dam-head of every one of the scores of mills in its course in what had been the highest flood since 1795. The River North Esk, also in flood, tore away the dam-head at Springfield and flooded parts of Lasswade.

Even today, the road over Soutra Hill can be troublesome in winter. In the days of horse-powered traffic, before the advent of snowploughs, snow often blocked the highway, with high winds also buffeting the traveller. In the seventeenth century, this road was:

"so worne and spoylled as hardlie is thair any journeying on horse or fuit... Bot with haisard and perrell".

For the benefit of those who do not understand seventeenth-century Scots, those words roughly translate as:

"So worn and spoiled that hardly anybody journeys on horse or foot except with hazard and peril."

Telford's upgraded road did not open until 1840, but his five-span Lothian Bridge at Pathhead is an architectural delight. The engineers of the nineteenth century were masters of their craft.

As well as the mediaeval hospital, in the nineteenth century, there was an inn at Lawrie's Den on Soutra. Unfortunately, that place earned a bit of a rough reputation as gypsies, drovers and other wandering men tended to congregate there, to the dismay of the more respectable traveller. Midlothian's roads were dotted with inns, for in the days before motor cars, people spent days on uncomfortable journeys that today would take only a few hours. As well as highways were the even poorer-maintained local roads and intricate farm-tracks that crossed and crisscrossed between the settlements, but there were occasions when bands of wanderers could cause consternation to the more remote communities and lone cottages miles into the more remote areas. These travelling or "gaun-aboot-folk" could be gypsies, tinkers or plain sorners. The gypsies, or Egyptians, arrived in Scotland in the late fifteenth or early sixteenth century, wanderers from India. The tinkers were reputed to be indigenous, the descendants of skilled metal workers from thousands of years ago, now with their social status sadly declined, while the sorners were plain trouble, bands of rogues, thieves and generally unpleasant people who infested the countryside.

Midlothian was also a land of grand estates and noble houses. Great landowners lived here; Ramsay of Dalhousie, Dundas of Arniston and the Duke of Buccleuch, who owned Dalkeith Palace. Even the High Court judge, Lord Cockburn contemplated buying the lovely Kirkhill by Gorebridge. In a letter to John Richardson in November 1808, Cockburn described Kirkhill as a "little spot... Ever sacred in my memory for its beauty and associations." The mansion houses also included Hawthornden, the one-time home of the poet William Drummond that sits beside the North Esk. Hawthornden was the object of the curious even in the eighteenth century when the Welsh traveller Thomas Pennant visited and recorded his impressions. Ben Jonson, the English dramatist, once walked from London to visit Drummond in Hawthornden, which shows the attraction of this literary figure.

However, such literary and historical tourism was not always popular with the locals: in the summer of 1859, a party of visitors from Fife came to visit Roslin and Hawthornden but strayed onto land owned by John Aitchison, who farmed nearby Mountmarle. The farmer attacked them, pushing the women and giving one of the men, Captain Blyth, a black eye. "I am sorry I am not prepared with arms," Captain Blyth said, "as I usually am when I go among savages."

In the nineteenth century, the towns were smaller and the villages and hamlets more self-contained. Even the smallest of settlements had butchers and bakers, with local work available at mines and quarries while there were also gunpowder mills at Gorebridge and Roslin, paper mills at Penicuik, a carpet factory at Lasswade and a busy farmer's market at Dalkeith. In the eighteenth century, there was a massive agricultural revolution that saw the open mediaeval run-rig farming system replaced by enclosed and drained fields, with planned villages and smart farm steadings replacing the old ferm-touns and dispossessing scores of families. One of these planned villages was Carlops in the lee of the Pentland Hills, created in 1784 and intended for cotton weaving, but a few decades later became a centre of woollen manufacture. It is a sleepy commuter village now, but then it would be alive with the clack of handlooms and vibrant with people who lived and worked within its confines.

Dalkeith was Midlothian's major market town but also seemed to be the magnet for many unwanted, with, in 1847, sixteen lodging houses of the worst description, situated in narrow, stinking closes in the parts of the town that visitors would be advised to avoid. Even the most luxurious of these penny-a-night haunts were only fourteen feet square, and held as many as eight beds, with perhaps one tiny window that was seldom opened and even more rarely washed. On a single night, one such room could hold eighteen men and women, plus a gaggle of children, with no prospect of privacy or comfort, thick air and the pervasive stink of unwashed bodies.

Pathhead, that lovely long village near the border with East Lothian (then Haddingtonshire), had an accumulation of lodging houses for the many wandering agricultural labourers. As so often at the time, the Irish, victims of terrible land management and famine, endured the worst conditions, with one building of five small rooms in Pathhead holding fifty adults. By 1844, Gorebridge also had a lodging house, with a desperate or unfortunate woman named Christina Boyd given ten days in jail in November that year for stealing clothes from other residents.

The wealthy were not always oblivious to the poverty of so many people and sometimes tried to help. For instance, in the hard winter of early 1832, Graeme Mercer, of Mavis Bank near Loanhead, opened a soup kitchen that supplied sixty-five people with soup and bread three days a week. Mercer seems to have been a caring man, for he also donated oatmeal and increased his regular annual gift of coal to the poor by an extra sixty tubs.

As a counterweight to the black poverty that many experienced, Midlothian was also a land of poets and story-tellers. As well as Drummond of Hawthornden, there was Sir Walter Scott who lived at Barony House, then known as Lasswade Cottage, from 1798 until 1804. James Hogg, the Ettrick Shepherd, visited him here, and the Wordsworths popped in to say hello and sample his hospitality. Robert Louis Stevenson spent much of his youth wandering the Pentland Hills from his base at Swanston and his first piece of writing concerned the 1666 Pentland Rising. Thomas de Quincy lived at Polton; he wrote *Confessions of an English Opium Eater*. Henry MacKenzie, who wrote *The Man of Feeling*, stayed in Auchendinny, with an exceptional view of the Pentland Hills. There was also at least one famous artist, with William McTaggart calling Lasswade home from 1889.

But always behind everything, there was agriculture and mining. Midlothian has some of the most fertile agricultural land in Scotland, if not in Britain, and the farms here are among the best run anywhere.

Midlothian Mayhem

It is possible to travel only ten or twelve miles from the capital and be in a different world. The area around Carrington is a rural idyll, while there are still corners of the Pentland hills where it is possible to spend many hours with only the call of the whaup and the soft sough of wind through the heather. To the outsider, farming seems peaceful and healthy, but it is, and always has been, a hard business to wrest a living from the soil in Scotland's climate. Working outside in all weathers, summer and winter, with fluctuating prices and always the fear that an overnight storm, frost or flood could ruin a year's work, farmers lived on the edge of poverty. Such a life made for hard men and sometimes the stress came out in an explosion of violence. However, there could also be moments of sublime beauty, if the beholder had the eye, and the leisure, to see. Here is a quote from a letter written by Lord Cockburn to Mrs John Richardson in April 1809:

> "I went up Torphin Hill ... Amidst the songs of two or three mavises who were perched on full-grown broom bushes. Several people were prolonging their field labours by sowing long after six- the smoke, symptomatic of rural porridge, ascended from the low-lying Collington... the first lambs were beginning to appear on the hills; it was so calm that the wheels of the solitary carts were heard on the Lanark road."

Reading that, Midlothian would seem a rural paradise, but Cockburn did not have to endure the achingly long hours behind the plough in often coarse weather.

Beneath the land is a tracery of tunnels from old mine workings. Mining was part of this land for centuries, with the monks of Newbattle lifting the "black stanis" from the twelfth century onward. When steam replaced water power, coal became king and propelled the second stage of the Industrial Revolution. Pits opened across the width and breadth of Midlothian, some small, some large and all providing laborious employment to dozens, scores and often hundreds of women, children and men. Various landowners sunk pits in their estates and took the profits to finance a lifestyle far removed from that of the workers who toiled in often terrible conditions far underground.

One of these landowners, the Marquis of Lothian, had a perfect pedigree for a coal master, being a descendant of Mark Ker, the last abbot of Newbattle. Naming one pit the Lady Victoria in honour of his wife, in the final decade of the nineteenth century the Marquis expanded Newtongrange into the most extensive mining village in Scotland. He had the streets placed in a grid pattern and gave them evocative names such as First Street, Second Street and Third Street. For the time, the houses were commodious, comfortable and well-built with local bricks; each had an outside toilet, which was advanced for the time, and came with a garden for vegetables. The Marquis's company, the Lothian Coal Company, also had a Miner's Institute with a library and reading room to offer the miners an alternative to spending all their leisure time in the pub, and there were bowling greens and football pitches. There was also a pub, run on the Gothenburg system, which was intended to discourage custom and leak profits back to the community.

At the time of writing, 2020, the industry has ended, with grassy mounds and declinations marking where pits once sunk deep into the earth. While some smaller mining settlements have vanished or are altered beyond recognition, others retain the appearance they had during their mining heyday. The most distinctive of these are the brick-built villages of Rosewell and Newtongrange – "Nitten" in local parlance. The latter settlement has various pieces of mining memorabilia placed around the streets, but most important is the excellent museum at the Lady Victoria Pit. The architecture and the museum serve as reminders of the centuries when men, women and children spent their working lives in the damp, dangerous dark underground.

As well as hard work in field, mill or mine, the possibility of disease was a constant fear. Smallpox hit Dalkeith in 1808, and the dreaded cholera epidemics of 1832 and 1848 created terror. There were also accidents at work, some of which could be quite spectacular, such as the explosions at Hitchener and Hunter's gunpowder work at Stobbs Mills in Gorebridge in February 1825. The first explosion was at the drying house when two men, Richard Cornwell, who had worked there for twenty-five years, and Walter Thomson, father of five children, had loaded up their wagon nearby. The explosion killed both men and flattened the drying house and its high chimney, ripped surrounding trees from the ground and lifted a four-ton boiler, to toss it fifteen yards away.

The explosion smashed all the windows in Hitchener's home, a quarter of a mile distant, and damaged nearly every house in Gorebridge. It was heard for a radius of twenty miles, knocked down travellers on the road a mile away, rang the church bells in Dalkeith and shook people in Haddington and North Berwick. As sixty 112-pound barrels of gunpowder blew up, a massive column of smoke rose skyward and drifted across the countryside, temporarily blotting out the sun. People from miles around rushed to try and help, congesting the roads with horses, carts and pedestrians.

That was bad enough but much worse was the Mauricewood mine disaster of September 1889, in which sixty-three men lost their lives. Mauricewood was in the Penicuik area, with seventy men working underground. On the day of the disaster, the wood lining caught fire and spread to the coal seam at which the colliers were working. The fire blocked all exits and men died either from smoke inhalation or were burned as they tried to run through the flames. Only seven men out of seventy made it to the surface, and it was four days before the fire was extinguished.

But Midlothian was not all about work and bad times. There was a surprising variety of sporting occupations in the fields and rolling hills, and in the days before professional sport with rigid regulations, some activities were a bit strange to our ears. For example, in July 1806, an East Lothian gentleman placed a wager that he could run the two and a half miles from the coal pits at his home in Musselburgh to Dalkeith within an hour: blindfolded. When the blindfold was applied, he set off, with the spectators either cheering or jeering, depending on which side they had placed their money. He managed the distance in an impressive forty minutes and pocketed five guineas for his trouble.

Sometimes the people could combine pleasure with the grim business of preparing for war. The first fifteen years of the nineteenth century were darkened by the long wars with Revolutionary and Napoleonic France, with the added complication of a short, sharp conflict with the United States of America between 1812 and early 1815. For much of that period, Midlothian, in common with the rest of Great Britain, could feel like an armed camp, with so many military uniforms on show. As well as the regulars there were Yeomanry and Volunteers, all in tunics that seemed to be designed to outshine each other in brilliance rather than be practical on the battlefield. Although these units were more likely to be used in aiding the civil powers, guarding prisoners-of-war or in helping keep down disturbances in Ireland, rather than facing the formidable French, they drilled enthusiastically and took part in military training.

On the 24th February 1804, the Midlothian based militia regiments staged what was known as a Grand Field Day with a "mock fight." With one brigade under Brigadier General Lord Dalhousie and the other under Sir James St Clair Erskine, they marched to the policies of Dalkeith Palace. Erskine's men defended the palace as Dalhousie's attacked in two lines, with musketry and cannon fire adding a background of loud noise and clouds of white smoke.

The main attack was on the bridge and stable-yard, which eventually fell to Dalhousie's gallant men with a loud British cheer and a flourish of the Union flag. There were eight thousand militiamen in this display of splendour, and an audience of the great and good that rolled up in their carriages to watch. The reality of blood and agony and splintered bodies was not present to spoil what the *Caledonian Mercury* described as "the brilliancy of the scene."

That French war finally ended in 1815, but the love of games, sport and pastimes did not. In the afternoon of Monday, the 19th February 1816, the people of Midlothian enjoyed a sight that few would have seen before and probably would never see again. A hot air balloon rose from the grounds of Mr Davidson's coach house in Dalkeith and cruised southward over the Moorfoot hills in multi-coloured splendour. Open-mouthed children and no-less-impressed adults stared at its passage as the balloon drifted south, not to descend until it reached Preston in Northumberland an hour and a half later. Such sights must have brightened the lives of men and women who toiled six days a week and welcomed night as a period of exhausted slumber.

Much more widespread was fox hunting, with the Midlothian Fox Hounds meeting at various locations throughout the county. For example, in the first week of December 1823, there were three meetings: at Houston Woods, at Newbattle and the windmill near Vogrie. In the 1840s, the Duke of Buccleuch's fox hounds favoured the Edmonstone and Crichton area, with one meeting in February 1846 following an unfortunate fox from Crichton dean to Mountskip to Roman Camp Hill and back to Vogrie, then south as far as the Gala Water, an 18-mile chase with an inevitably gory end.

Blood sports continued with the Midlothian Coursing Club, whose members hunted for hares. In November 1844 the autumn meeting of the club was somewhat disappointing, as, despite a plethora of eager dogs and even more excited owners, coarse weather, in the form of rain and sleet, spoiled the hunting and made hares scarce. The third meet of the season was on the Marquis of Lothian's land at Roman Camp Hill, the haunt of Camp Meg, who was keen on that sport. Other members included the august Lord Douglas, Wardlaw Ramsay of Whitehill and Sir Graham Montgomery.

Curling was also much more popular then than now, with outdoor rinks across Midlothian. In some ways, it was Scotland's national sport before organised football burst onto the scene in the last decades of the nineteenth century. For example, on the last Friday in January 1847, three rinks of the Dalkeith curling club played three of the East Linton Club at the pond at Gladsmuir. Perhaps surprisingly, cricket was also a favourite Scottish sport, with the students of Loretto School hammering the Dalkeith Cricket Club in 1859.

Less salubrious to modern tastes was the sport of dogfighting. Coalcarters were among the roughest characters on the roads, with a reputation for dishonesty and casual violence. Many of them also kept fighting dogs, with bull mastiffs being their favoured breed. Any traveller passing their carts had to walk warily in case the dogs attacked them, and anybody with their own pet dog was well advised to keep clear, for the carters' bulldogs would strike without warning. In April 1828, one man, named Robert Wilson, was walking near Dalkeith when a pack of carters' dogs lunged at his black pointer. Luckily, Wilson carried a small two-barrelled pistol; he shot and killed one dog and wounded another. Before he could reload, the carters had gathered and ran at him, fists pounding and metal-studded boots kicking. Happily, Wilson was as adept with his feet as he was with his pistol; he turned and ran, outdistancing the carters and their dogs.

There were also athletic meetings, such as the Roslin Games. In August 1840, nearly three thousand people gathered in Roslin Glen, with the newly formed County Police there to make sure there was no major trouble. The sports included quoits and rifle shooting, throwing the hammer, putting the 22-pound weight, high jump and races, including a spectacular steeplechase that included a splashing ford over the Esk. There was quite an interest in these local games, with the July event that same year in Dalkeith attracting ten thousand people, so that gentlemen such as Wardlaw Ramsay of Whitehill rubbed shoulders with colliers and farmers as they competed at archery. The other games were similar to those at Roslin, with the addition of wrestling.

Despite all the opportunities for healthy exercise, probably the most popular pastime in nineteenth-century Midlothian was visiting the local public house. There were many "publics" and inns in the villages and along the highways, and all the evidence suggests that local people were not backward in patronising them. Drink features in many, if not most, of the crimes of violence in the nineteenth century, and well-founded fears about the levels of drinking led to the temperance movements. Alcohol was not a vice limited to any particular class. In his book, *Circuit Journeys* Lord Cockburn, who was to become a High

Court judge and who moved in the most elite circle of society, wrote about his first experience of an inn as a boy. It is an eye-opening introduction to the reality of life and how the elite could mix in democratic conviviality with ordinary people.

With the episode, centred in the Inn at Middleton, Cockburn said that the Duke of Buccleuch, Henry Dundas the Home Secretary and Viscount Melville, Robert Dundas of Arniston, the Lord Advocate, Hepburn of Clerkington "and several of the rest of the aristocracy of Midlothian… Congregated in this wretched inn." Cockburn said they were "roaring and singing, and laughing, in a low-roofed room, scarcely large enough to hold them, with wooden chairs and a sanded floor." They drank claret and a bowl of hot whisky punch, "while the odour was enough to perfume the whole parish," with the men "all in a state of elevation, although there was nothing like absolute intoxication… Enjoying their unchecked boose." It is a reminder that at that period, as in all periods, there were happy times as well as sad.

Another example proving that the highest could mix with the less exalted occurred in June 1832, after the passing of the Great Reform Bill. There was a significant gathering in Dalkeith, with flags and trade banners and clamorous bands. Ignoring the rain, around 1,200 people marched down the High Street to the entrance of Dalkeith Palace, turned right past the Wheat Market to Back Street and South Street to the High Street again. They paraded outside the Town House, with around forty flags of various incorporations. The slogans and mottos on the banners were like a clarion call of political triumph. Among others, there were banners from the Reform Committee, Shoemakers, Tailors, Carters and the Stobshill Colliers.

The Tailors' banner read:

> Behold the dawn of freedom's dawn
> The Bakers' banner read:
> With joy we hail the glorious morn
> that beams the tidings of reform.'

There was a great deal of cheering for Earl Grey who forced through the bill and for King William the reformer, with rolling of drums and firing of muskets. By the end of the meeting, there were five thousand people in the pouring rain and not a whisper of trouble.

So that is a quick pen picture of Midlothian in the eighteenth and nineteenth century. It was a county of contrasts, of fertile farms and hidden mines, of markets and hills, of very hard-working people and half-forgotten history, of bad roads and enormous potential. It was a place where poverty clung in the shade of wealth, men and women struggled in the dark underground, misery hid behind the bold scarlet of military uniforms and crime waited in the dark shadows. It was also a place where people made the best of what they had.

Chapter 2

THE COLLIERS: FIGHTING FOR FREEDOM

Life as a collier was hard, brutal, dirty and often short. There was danger all around, in the toxic air, in the creaking rock above, in the water that could flood the pits and in the dust that they breathed. Worse, until 1799 the colliers could be bought and sold with the pits; they were serfs as bound to the pit as any Russian peasant was tied to the land.

The monks at Newbattle were the first recorded Scots to mine coal, making the Midlothian pits the oldest known in the country. The coal industry continued throughout the Middle Ages, with salters and limemakers using the fuel as well as housewives and servants in grand castles. By the middle of the sixteenth century, Scottish colliers hacked out about 40,000 tons of coal a year, so it was immensely valuable to the Scottish economy as well as keeping the people warm in the long dreich winters. As coal-masters and landowners exploited this black wealth, they needed a labour force, and as they exhausted supplies of coal near the surface, they sunk pits deeper and deeper into the ground. Naturally, the further the pits sunk, the greater the danger, with gas, fire, flooding and cave-ins all of massive concern to the miners.

Some of the best minds of the age concentrated on making the pits more efficient, although more for the sake of the owner's profit than out of concern for the sweating men and near-naked women who toiled in the guts of the earth. Towards the end of the sixteenth century, John Napier of Merchiston, the genius who created logarithms to torment generations of school children, invented a pump to clear water from coal mines, but the major problem of labour remained. Nobody wanted to work in the hellish conditions underground.

In 1606, three years after he added the crown of England to his hereditary title of King of Scots, James Stuart re-introduced slavery to Scotland. It may have been called collier-serf, or just serf, but to all intents and purposes the Scottish colliers, together with the salters, were enslaved. By taking this inhuman step, King James VI guaranteed the mine owners a permanent, skilled workforce. He was not suddenly out of step with Scots Law, however, but had only taken another stride in the degradation of the more impoverished Scots that had continued for some time. James's great grandfather, King James IV, had ordered that beggars be grabbed and sent to sea in fishing boats, while the Scots Poor Law of 1579 said that vagrants could be whipped, branded or given in a year-long servitude to an employer. The vagrant's children could be put into bondage until they were twenty-four if male and eighteen if they were female. Twenty years later, children of vagrants and vagrants themselves, could be placed in servitude for life. Although very few Parish Kirk Sessions lowered themselves to utilising this law, the fact that it was in place enabled the Coal Masters full scope to enslave any colliers that worked for them.

Why were there so many vagrants at this period? Partly because of religious changes, for the onset of Protestantism saw the destruction of the monasteries with consequent losses of employment to all who had worked there, and partly because of a period of bad weather. From around 1570 the earth cooled, disrupting harvests and causing famine. People left the land that could no longer feed them, while others sought food from their neighbours – it is no coincidence that the last decades of the sixteenth century saw a spike in clan wars in the Scottish Highlands and along the Border with England. Communities desperate for food would have no qualms in sending their young men out to steal the cattle from a neighbouring clan.

With King James pushing to increase Scottish industry and fully approving of their actions, the Lords of the Articles, the Scottish parliament, passed the 1606 Act that nailed colliers and salters into bondage. The Act had five main provisions. Nobody could hire colliers, coal-bearers or salters without written permission from their master. If any collier, coal-bearer or salter left his position without such consent, his master could claim him back, as long as it was within a year and a day. If the collier, bearer or salter had a new employer, that man was legally bound to hand him over. Any workman who left his owner's employment without permission was legally a thief as he had stolen away his own body, which was owned by his master.

As if that was not power enough, the Act also enabled coal-masters and salt masters to kidnap any vagabond or "sturdy beggar" they saw and enslave him in their works.

It is perhaps not surprising that coal-masters were among the lords of the Privy Council, who helped enforce this abominable Act. In 1641, with two wars between Covenanted Scotland and King Charles completed and another threatening, the Scottish Parliament strengthened the Act, saying the mine workers had too many holidays at "which times they employ in drinking and debauchery to the great offence of God and prejudice of their master." From that date, colliers had to work six days a week with minimum holidays. Six years later, the Christmas, "Yule" holiday was removed as being "superstitious." It was from the time of the Covenanters that the Christmas holiday was downgraded in Scotland, with New Year becoming more important.

The Acts continued, tightening the screw so that, in 1661, colliers who failed to work their allotted six days a week had to pay a twenty-shillings Scots fine to their master for each day they did not work, plus face corporal punishment. In Preston Grange, and possibly elsewhere, as late as the eighteenth century, erring colliers could be placed in the jougs or "made to go the rown," which meant being tied facing the horse at the gin and forced to run backwards all day. To pile on the insults, colliers were not included in the Scottish Habeas Corpus Act of 1701, or rather the Act "for preventing wrong imprisonment."

Scottish colliers took what was known as "arles" or earnest-money as he was bound to a master, and worse, it became the norm for a man to sell his son or daughter into the same slavery. Although the males were paid for their labour, their daughters or wives were not. They were the coal-bearers, the people who had the terrible task of carrying coal, a hundredweight or more at a time, from the coal face to the pit bottom through often-flooded, low-ceilinged "bearer's ways" and up flights of rickety ladders. If a man had no wife to do this labour, he had to pay to hire a woman, which makes one wonder how many marriages were for convenience rather than romance. Given the life that they had, it is unlikely that love was of vital importance to the colliers.

It is only human nature that when one type or class of person is treated differently to others, the mass of the population should also look down upon them. That is what happened to the colliers. Often living in small villages apart from other people, usually dirty from labouring, and with women and children also working, colliers were not the most refined of people. Other people, decent in all other ways, avoided the colliers, who were even kept separate in church. A pamphlet of 1793, *Considerations on the Present Scarcity and High Price of Coals* in Scotland, claimed the colliers were "destitute of all principles of religion and morality" they "lived in dirty hovels, a few loose boards and straw formed their beds, a pot and pan, with round stones, or timber stools to sit on, the whole furniture of the house." The colliers were also slated for making their wives and daughters "carry coals on their backs" and for "mixing the sexes in the pits."

As for being destitute of all principles of religion and morality, Newton Parish Church has evidence to the contrary. Newton is the parish north of Dalkeith and in the eighteenth century already boasted a strong tradition of coal mining. In 1725 the colliers or "colhewers belonging to Mr Biggar" asked the Kirk Session if they could have their own section – called a loft – inside the church. The Session agreed on the condition that the landowner, John Wauchope of Edmonstown, was in favour, so it took until 1732 for the agreement to come through. The colliers did not have many years to enjoy their loft, for a new church was erected in 1742, although a colliers' loft was added five years later. Ironically for the House of God where all are equal, the colliers had to climb a staircase on the exterior of the church to get to their loft, no doubt for fear of contaminating the more apparently respectable members of the congregation.

Throughout this time, the Coal Masters retained the power to enslave vagrants, although evidence for that happening appears scanty. However, there is no doubt that bands of the homeless or just plain wanderers continued to upset rural communities, as this small piece from the *Aberdeen Press and Journal* of the 21st of July 1752 proves:

> "Edinburgh, five vagrants, two men and three women were brought in from Dalkeith to Edinburgh tolbooth."

As the eighteenth century wore on, the colliers were becoming restless, or perhaps their restlessness was better recorded. In October 1743, fifteen colliers from the pits at Gilmerton, then a few miles south of Edinburgh, decided to leave the works. As most of the men had been bred as colliers and knew no other occupation, the owner, Sir John Baird of Newbyth, one-time MP for Edinburghshire, and a man with all the privileges of a baronet, could not understand their reasoning. Nor did he have any sympathy. Instead, he was implicit in the orders to other Coal Masters to "seize and apprehend them… so they may be incarcerated." David Baird of the same family, an Edinburgh merchant, offered half a guinea reward to anybody who captured any of the runaways. What was worse for Sir John, another nine colliers joined the initial fifteen. The Lord Justice Clerk aided Sir John by issuing a warrant to arrest the colliers.

By May 1749 the gentlemen Coal Masters were becoming increasingly concerned about their colliers' behaviour. They decided it would be advantageous to have regular meeting to have a mutual understanding to work out measures "for keeping their colliers in subjection." Such combinations were unlawful for workers, but seemed to be accepted, if created by Coal Masters.

The drift away from coal mines continued, with three of Sir William Dalrymple's colliers at Cranston departing without permission in July 1749, "after very great crimes," according to the authorities. Two months later, there was another meeting of the gentleman Coal Masters where they voiced their determination to prosecute anybody who gave employment to "vagrant and runaway colliers" who should be "sent back to their proper master."

In November 1750, the colliers around Alloa were so troublesome that the authorities sent four companies of infantry to keep them in order. In Midlothian, the discontent seemed less organised, but there were undoubtedly unhappy people as a man named David Irvine tried to set fire to Sir James Clerk's coal pits at Loanhead. The sheriff had him grabbed and placed in jail, where he remained for some time before being freed with stern commands never to come within half a mile of the pits again.

Other colliers proved the unrest with their behaviour, such as the men of Andrew Wallace's Woolmot colliery. In January 1762, when a collier named William Bennet spoke out against the work practices, Wallace ordered him arrested. Francis Frazer, a sheriff officer, came out to Bennet's home, at which point Bennet's workmates rose in a body, grabbed Frazer and took away his warrant. Wallace, backed by the local sheriff and magistrates, took things a step further by sending in the cavalry. A troop of light horse clattered into the area, arrested fifteen colliers and dragged them to Edinburgh, where they were thrown into the Tolbooth, the notorious Heart of Midlothian that served as the city jail.

In 1762, the colliers across Scotland prepared to apply to parliament for their freedom. The leaders of the colliers met at Mrs Walker's Inn in Edinburgh on Friday, the 1st of October. To their credit, some of the Coal Masters and tacksmen – the mine managers - supported the colliers; others, however, did not.

By that time, with Britain locked in the Seven Years War with France, coal was rising in price. The Coal Masters and colliers each blamed the other for the increase. In March 1762, a meeting of the "Gentlemen Coal Masters" announced that the "high price of coal" was owing to the "idleness, mutinous disposition and extravagant wages of the colliers." Encouraging this evil, apparently, were these men who gave work to "all vagrant colliers" so the Gentlemen Coal Masters resolved not to employ any collier without a proper certificate from his legal master.

What the Coal Masters termed as "vagrant colliers" were the men who voted with their feet, leaving what were probably horrendous workplaces to search for better conditions. The Coal Masters frequently placed advertisements in the local newspapers warning of these vagrants, such as this one placed in the *Caledonian Mercury* on 23rd April 1764:

> *Whereas William Ross, Thomas Cunningham, Andrew Wilson and Robert Thomson, colliers, have lately deserted Hawthorndean colliery; and whereas Alexander Sneddon, Robert Brown and William Muir likewise colliers, threaten to do the same, although they are all bound by contract to serve the proprietor thereof till the middle of November next, and to give two months warning before they leave him, therefore Dr Abernethy-Drummond gives this public notice to all gentleman coal-masters and tacksmen of collieries in order that none of them may harbour or give encouragement to such deserters. And if any person other than their proper Masters shall, notwithstanding of this intimation, receive any of the above-named colliers, he may depend upon being prosecuted according to law, meantime, if the colliers will return to their work at Hawthornden, their past behaviour shall be forgiven.*

As well as deserting their servitude, the colliers tried to improve their condition by encouraging the Coal Masters to raise their wages. It is possible they formed a combination, for the Midlothian Coal Masters met in John's coffeehouse in Edinburgh on the 21st of June 1764 to combat this illegal action.

The colliers retaliated with their own meetings and notices in the press such as this one from the *Caledonian Mercury* of 25th March 1769

> *As the Scheme at present in agitation for obtaining freedom to the Colliers upon a just and proper footing, so as the interest of no party may be prejudiced, and the police of the country thereby improved is an object of general and important concern; this is to give notice, that though the laying before the public a fuller account of the intended proceedings for the above laudable purpose, has been hitherto delayed, yet from the progress already made, it is hoped the same will soon be done ; and it is in the meantime expected, that the meetings at Walter Laidlaw's in Dalkeith, will be continued the first Saturday of every month, where the Colliers and all others concerned will attend to contribute, and to give such instructions and hints as they may think proper for promoting the above scheme.*

On 29th August 1772 the Midlothian colliers, together with the salters, again resolved to petition parliament for their freedom. Despite the wishes of many Coal Masters to maintain the status quo, the Royal Boroughs of Scotland saw the sense of the petition, and gave their proposals for gradual liberty for the colliers.

In 1774 a parliamentary Bill partially alleviated the conditions of colliers and salters. King George III gave his royal assent that same year so that from the 1st July 1775, the colliers would gradually be freed but with stringent conditions. The younger men, those not yet twenty, had to work a further seven years before they were released. Men of twenty-one but not yet thirty-five had to work an additional ten years, while those between thirty-five and forty-five had only seven years with a proviso that the collier had to have instructed an apprentice in "the art or mystery of coal-hewing." If the collier failed to provide an apprentice on the master's orders, he had to work another three years. Men over forty-five – and these were reckoned old – were immediately set free. If any man took part in a strike to raise wages or left their master's service early, they were sentenced to a further two years servitude.

It was freedom of a sort, with the colliers celebrating the 1st July as a holiday thereafter.

Once the collier was freed, his wife and children automatically shook off their shackles. However, although the Act meant well, the provisos made it virtually impossible for the majority of colliers to obtain their freedom. Probably the most significant hurdle was the interesting little clause that stated the collier had to take his master to the Sheriff Court to prove his right to escape from serfdom. Such a course must have been incredibly daunting, while it was also true that many of the colliers were in debt to their masters. Some of the Coal Masters ensured that the colliers continued in debt by operating a "truck" system, which meant the masters sold necessities to their workers at high prices, often driving the men and women into debt which could never be repaid. As the colliers often lived in villages a distance from markets and were too exhausted to travel after work, the advantages always lay with the Coal Masters.

As the colliers celebrated the illusion of freedom that the government had dangled before them, their life continued much as before, with danger, toil and oppression. There were also advertisements for colliers and bearers, with one placed in January 1796, where Mr Dewar of Vogrie also searched for a grieve (an overseer) "whose character for attention and honesty must bear the strictest enquiry."

Towards the end of the eighteenth century, the world was changing. First, the United States struggled free of Britain's imperial grasp to establish itself as a vigorous republic, and then the French people discarded their king and nobility in the celebration of slaughter that history has termed the French Revolution. In the British Isles, there was further discontent, with the United Irishmen rising in Ireland, militia riots in Scotland, the United Scotsmen causing unease among the ruling elite, and mutiny in the Navy, Britain's wooden-walled guardians.

Augmenting all these troubles was a not-particularly-successful war with France and her satellite states and an increasing demand for coal to fuel the industrialisation of the nation. The Coal Masters retained their grip on their semi-servile workforce. Hewing and carrying coal were labour intensive, and very few people would wish to work in shocking conditions, even for good money.

Finally, the colliers were becoming ever more militant. Perhaps because they knew they were near-outsiders in their own country, they joined together to increase their strength. The author of *Considerations on the Present Scarcity and High Price of Coal in Scotland* wrote that the colliers had a practice called "brotherings: It is a solemn oath… to stand by each other." This early form of trades union worried the Coal Masters, who knew that their wealth depended on the labour of their workers.

It may have been the Coal Masters who influenced the press against the colliers, so that in October 1792 the *Caledonian Mercury* printed an article about the scarcity of coal in the Edinburgh neighbourhood. Stating that the lack of coal "bears peculiarly hard on the poorer rank of citizens," the piece puts the blame squarely on "a want of colliers; numbers of whom have deserted the service" although "colliers make better wages than most tradesmen."

Such attacks on the colliers continued as the Coal Masters sought to retain their grip on their workforce. In May 1799, the colliers retaliated with their own piece in the press, saying that the 'malicious reports' about the colliers having 'been the cause of raising the price of coals' were 'false and ill-founded.' They added, quite truthfully, that 'it is not in the power of the colliers to raise their own wages or the price of coal.' The writer also mentions that the Coal Masters and others had been claiming that colliers were "remarkable for idleness and immorality and a lawless and disorderly class of people" and said that was "a rash and groundless charge as can be attested by both Magistrates and Ministers in the Lothians." The composer ended with a Biblical reference to completely throw off the attackers: "if the persons who have circulated these misrepresentations would first take the beam from their own eyes they would see the clearer to take the mote out of theirs."

As this verbal warfare continued, the colliers eventually won their freedom. On 13th June 1799, the government finally ended serfdom but with a clause in the Act that outlawed combinations, or trades unions. As before, the Coal Masters tried to stop the bill, and as before, the government, to their credit, overturned their objections. The colliers had won; they were as free as any other labourers in Scotland. No longer bound to their masters, no longer forced to work underground with the weight of the earth above them, many left the pits and sought alternative employment. Others remained, still with the danger and hardships of the mines, but now as free men and free women.

Chapter 3

FIGHTING FOR IMPROVEMENT

Derby Mercury, 26th February 1747:

> *Last Week a melancholy accident happened at a Coal-Pit two Miles from Dalkeith; the Overseer, with four of the Colliers, having gone down suspecting there was a Fire in the Pit, were all suffocated with the Smoak in a few Minutes. We hear the Pit continues burning.*

The colliers' working life was unpleasant at best. Bonded or free, there was no escaping from the hardship or danger that surrounded colliers and their families, without even the consolation of a decent home in which to relax at the end of their shift.

To taste a flavour of these bad old days, find a copy of the Children's Employment Commission report of 1842, over forty years after the ending of slavery, so things had theoretically improved. The often-heart-rending accounts by young children will chill the blood and make the reader wonder at the price ordinary people had to pay for the Industrial Revolution that set Britain to the forefront of the world, and to keep the landowners in fancy clothes and fine food.

There was Janet Cummings, for example. She was an eleven-year-old child who went down the pit at five in the morning with the other women, and returned at five at night. She was a coal-bearer, carrying creel-loads of a hundredweight and more underground, wading calf-deep in cold water. Sir John Hope of Pinkie owned the pit and profited from her labour.

George Reid was sixteen and said he had to "twist myself up" to work on the 26- inch high coal seam. He had started work below aged ten years, and most days only ate bread and drank the stagnant water in the pit. He told the Commission that "there is a good deal of quarrelling below, especially among the women people."

Twelve-year-old George King started work when he was aged eight. He left home at two in the morning and sometimes worked until six at night. "I have sometimes been belted," he said, taking such things in his stride, "as most boys are."

Twelve-year-old George Jamieson picked coal and spoke about his domestic arrangements. He said that "we have one room in our house and two beds, two sisters and the three laddies sleep in one bed and mother and father in the other."

Phillis Flockhart was a twelve-year-old road clearer, entering the pits at night to mend the walls and ensure the roads are clear for the bearers. "I am a natural child," she said, "mother left me when three years of age."

There are many more examples, some heart-breaking, others tinged with hope, but all demonstrating that life was hard for adults and children. Men toiled underground, often lying on their sides in terribly uncomfortable positions as they hacked at narrow seams, with girls and women dragging the coal away or climbing ladders while carrying creels of a hundredweight and more on their backs. There was always the fear of "bad air" or cave-ins, with accidents common and early death likely. The job was as dangerous for women as it was for men, with, for example, seventeen-year-old Agnes Moffat mentioning to the 1842 Commission:

"The work is o'er sair for females; had my shoulder knocked out a short time ago, idle some time. It is no' uncommon for women to lose their burthen and drop off the ladder down below; Margaret M'Neil did a few weeks since, and injured both legs. When the tugs which pass over the forehead break, which they frequently do, it is very dangerous to be under a load."

Sixteen-year-old Helen Reid gave her own story: "Two years since the pit closed upon thirteen of us and we were two days without food or light; nearly one day we were up to our chins in water. At last we got to an old shaft, which we picked our way and were heard by people watching above. All were saved.

Two months ago I was filling the tubs at the pit bottom when the gig clicked too early, and the hook caught me by my pit clothes - the people did not hear my shrieks - my hand had fast grappled the chain, and the great height of the shaft caused me to lose my courage and I swooned, - the banksman could scarcely remove my hand, the deadly grasp saved my life."

Joseph Fraser, a 37-year old man, who worked in the Duke of Buccleuch's pits, said he had worked underground since he was ten. He said he had been married eighteen years and six of his eight children were still alive. Unlike most colliers, he did not allow his wife to work underground when she was pregnant, but "That is not the usual practice with men, who too frequently marry women for their labour than any liking they may have."

He added that women who worked underground married early, had large families, "and the children are as much neglected as they have been themselves." Fraser believed that because women worked underground, the men had no reason to go home. Instead they "drink hard… in time the women follow the men and drink hard also." Many women "work till the ninth month of pregnancy and frequently go home and bear the child. The work cause swelled joints and hips, and few women are fit for work after 35: even men drop off on the average before 40, especially where they live in damp houses. The asthma kills men quickly."

Even after freedom, rigid contracts bound the colliers; if they broke them, their masters could have them imprisoned. For instance, in September 1802, the sheriff at Dalkeith ordered a miner named William Hogg to six months solitary confinement for "deserting his service." He was to be fed only bread and water for three months of that time.

Danger waited in silent gas, known as "bad air," in roaring fires or the always-present fear of a cave-in, such as the one in Loanhead in October 1753, when the "pillars of a coal work gave way," injuring several men and, according to the *Caledonian Mercury* "one bruised in such manner that there are but small hopes of his recovery."

There were also other dangers, such as the accident that occurred in the Earl of Roseberry's Barley Dean Colliery in Carrington in September 1832. As so often in the mining industry, sons followed fathers down the pit and five sons of a man named William Penman worked there. All six had been working underground, and when the shift finished, William and two of his sons surfaced first. The other three were in the bucket, being raised to the top when the ring from which the rope to the bucket broke.

William could only watch in horror as three of his sons fell nearly two hundred feet into the darkness. He could do nothing to help, and one of his surviving sons descended to the bottom and got the mangled remains of his brothers back to the surface. It was as sudden and horrible as that.

There is no doubt that, in the nineteenth-century, coal mining was one of the most dangerous civilian occupations a man – or woman - could do. Second, only to a fisherman, a collier had one of the highest expectations of an accident at work. As well as the well-publicised major accidents where many men died in underground accidents, there was a constant dribble of incidents where colliers were injured or maimed.

As another example, on the 14th May 1823, a massive lump of rock fell from the roof of the pit at Vogrie Coal Work. It landed on top of one of the workers, Isabella Black, killing her instantly. It took four men to free her, including Isabella's father, for she was a mere ten years old and that was only her second day working underground.

With men, women and children existing in atrocious conditions, it was not surprising that the colliers hoped to improve their lives by fighting back. As individuals, they could not compete with entrenched, educated authority that both made the laws and enforced them. However, by collecting into combinations, they could withdraw their labour, thus hitting the Coal Masters in the only places they were vulnerable: their wallets and their sense of superiority.

After the French Revolution and the wars that ended in 1815, the Scottish and British establishment lived in fear of any dissent from the working people, the dispossessed mass of the population. Draconian laws were passed to keep the elite in power and subdue any show of dissent by the ordinary people. Although the authorities strictly enforced the Combination Acts of 1799 and 1800, in 1817 the colliers in the West of Scotland still managed to form a combination, or union. This union did not last long, but it showed a flame, however weak, that offered hope for a better future. That hope was needed, for the decade immediately after Waterloo was as grim as any in British history. As soon as the post-war boom subsided, unemployment and poverty struck hard, augmented by the thousands of suddenly unemployed soldiers and sailors who swarmed town and countryside desperate for work.

People groaned under an unfair electoral system that was as corrupt as any third-world country of today, with the authorities condemning those seeking to increase the franchise and make it more inclusive as Radicals. The government stamped with pitiless force, fuelled by fear, on the Radical's attempts to achieve more equality. However, some things slowly improved as the years turned, and in 1824 the Combination acts were repealed. The people stirred, trying everything they could, both within, and sometimes outside, the law to improve their lot.

Histories of the nineteenth century often mention the Chartists, who instituted one of the most extensive working-class movements in

Britain and were instrumental in the most extensive and widespread strike of the period. They were known as the Chartists because they signed the People's Charter, a document that asked for political reform through six major points:

> A vote for every man over 21 (rather than only the upper and middle classes.)
> Secret ballots (to end the corruption of public voting when the elite could evict or intimidate those who voted against them.)
> Pay for MPs (so ordinary people could afford to become Members of Parliament rather than only the wealthy.)
> Equal voting constituencies (to end the scandal of "rotten boroughs" where some MPs represented constituencies of a handful of people, and others served entire cities.)
> Annual elections
> MPs did not have to own property (another attempt to bring ordinary people into parliament.)

The Chartists were born in the wake of what was meant to be a reform to end any further agitation. For decades, people in Scotland, as in the other nations of the United Kingdom, had been stirring for political improvement. The old system was corrupt, with far too few people enjoying the franchise and, in Scotland, power firmly in the hands of a few wealthy landowners and their friends. In the late eighteenth century, with the French Revolution following that of the United States, people demanded political reform. In 1792, when people realised how corrupt the British system was, they burned effigies of Henry Dundas, the so-called "uncrowned king of Scotland" or "Old Corruption" whose statue now glowers over Edinburgh from St. Andrews Square. In Midlothian, a mob marched to his country seat of Melville Castle, which he gained when he married Elizabeth Rannie. The crowd might have destroyed the castle, had a troop of cavalry not trotted from Dalkeith to turn them back. Although Henry Dundas was one of the most important figures of his time, most people have forgotten him now.

The wars with France pushed political reform to the side in Scotland, and not until after victory at the Battle of Waterloo in 1815 did it properly rear its head again. The Great Reform Bill of 1832 increased the franchise tremendously, so many people the length and breadth of the country greeted it with great celebration, but while it included many of the middle classes, the 1832 Act excluded the working class entirely. With the industrial revolution bringing working people together as never before, in large factories and mills, in great urban conurbations and an increasing number of mines as steam power demanded coal, working-class organisation increased. Unions of workers began to campaign for better working conditions and more security. The alliance of political unity with the Chartists and integration with the combinations created a new dynamism that the authorities thought dangerous.

In 1839, the Chartists were at the centre of an outbreak of violence in Newport in Wales, where the army shot twenty-two men. After that, the authorities tended to react speedily and with force to the threat of any further worker-employer confrontation. After the heady years of the 1830s came the Hungry Forties, one of the most troubled decades of the century. It was a decade blighted by bad weather and poor harvests, by starvation and turmoil, a decade that saw the failure of crops across Northern Europe, governments in disarray and crowned heads toppling from Austria to France. In Britain, the "plug riots" of 1842, sometimes known as the General Strike heralded what was to be a troublesome few years. The name Plug Riots came from the fact that plugs or bolts were removed from steam engines so they would not work and the factory owners could not call in any strike-breaking labour.

This often-neglected piece of history started when parliament rejected a considerable petition that supported the Chartists' demands with something like contempt. When mill owners imposed wage cuts to add desperation to misery, the workers reacted. The coal miners of Staffordshire were first out when the Coal Masters cut their wages, and the discontent spread north and south to become the longest general strike in British political history. At its peak, it affected something like half a million men from Cornwall to Dundee, with mines, mills and factories closed and striking workmen standing idle on street corners and huddled in the corners of fields. At that period there were memories of the French Revolution when the workers caused the downfall of a dynasty that resulted in two decades of war, and more recent memories of the Scottish Radical War of 1820, so the government came down hard on any sign of unrest. In Preston, the military opened fire on a riot, with four men killed. The authorities killed six more men in Halifax, and there were further riots throughout Yorkshire, and the authorities arrested around 1,500 in north-west England. The dispute was not about significant political alterations: the workers only wanted their original wages restored and a ten-hour working day. In this case, the Charter seems to have been a supporting act: significant but marginal to the real problem.

The road to democracy, then, was turbulent, with the ruling classes holding on to power and repressing political progress with the bayonet and the Law that they had written to protect their interests. With Chartists among the leaders of the strike, the government responded with military force, sending the 34th and 73rd Foot to the disturbed north of England. According to folk tales, some of the soldiers refused to fire on the workers and were themselves arrested.

The Midlothian miners joined the general strike and clung on to the idea that they might make the government or the employers change their mind. Unfortunately, one major weakness of the strikers' position was a lack of resources. Once the strike began, wages naturally dried up, and immediately that happened, there was nothing left to pay the bills and feed the family.

In August 1842 there were rumours of trouble with the miners in the Dalkeith area. There had already been trouble in Tranent, and the authorities were afraid that the same might happen in Midlothian. The sheriff came in person to Dalkeith, bringing a bodyguard of police with him. For a while, Dalkeith saw a heavy police presence, with blue-coated constables with swallow-tailed coats and long staffs patrolling the usually quiet streets. As it happened, the Midlothian colliers caused no trouble at all on this occasion. The dispute was over wages and involved the men who worked for the Duke of Buccleuch, the Marquis of Lothian, Wardlaw Ramsay of Whitehill, Sir John Hope and Dundas of Arniston. One thousand five hundred colliers came into Dalkeith to discuss the possibility of a strike. In honour of the occasion, they wore their best clothes, and some carried ornate walking sticks. The gathering was very purposeful, with respectable men who appointed a miner from Wardlaw Ramsay's mines as chairman before they discussed their grievances.

There was a moment's tension when one of the men tried to expand the meeting to include Chartist demands, but the new chairman slapped him back down. Unfortunately, others at the meeting backed the heckler; the chairman was deposed and replaced with one with more Chartist views. After a further meeting, the miners agreed to a strike.

At a further meeting at West Houses in Newbattle, committee members from pits in East and West Lothian met with local men. There was anger when the miners of the Marquis of Lothian's Easter Bryans declared they did not intend to strike. A few of the more militant colliers reacted with threats against Lothian's mines, saying they would destroy not only the mine engines but also the houses in which the miners lived. The marquis and the sheriff decided that such threats could not be allowed, and swore in a dozen Special Constables. Specials were typically local men from a respectable background, who backed the authorities without benefit of pay. The authorities split their forces, stationing stationed pairs of Specials at Easthouses, West Houses, Gowkshill, Bryans Coalhill, and Newtongrange, with the final pair ordered to patrol the roads that connected the mining villages in case of troublesome gatherings. The specials were duty-bound to remain on station as long as the strike continued.

The miners had another meeting at New Craighall where Midlothian colliers disagreed whether to strike or not. Still divided, the miners gathered again at Edgehead, where political agitators presented large placards that included the slogan "People's Charter." The authorities responded with posters that announced that Queen Victoria had ordered measures to repress what they termed as "disturbances."

In mid-September, the miners published details of wages paid at seventeen different mines throughout Mid and East Lothian. They pointed out that at Edgehead and Huntlaw, the highest pay was twenty two shillings and sixpence a week for a fourteen-hour working day. Although that was good pay for the period, the gross total diminished when colliers had to pay the putters as well as buying their tools. A putter was the boy or girl who pushed a small four-wheeled cart with around three to five hundredweight of coal. At Tranent in East Lothian, the miner earned ten shillings at the top, and after paying the putter, oil and tools, he had a little over two shillings a week. The other collieries were between these figures. Naturally, the mine managers and others denied that wages were so low and claimed that in Newbattle alone, the net payments, after deductions, were nine shillings and a penny. The colliers put the figure at three shillings and sixpence.

In late September, as the strike wore on, the miners called another meeting at the Freemasons Hall in Dalkeith. Miners marched to the town from the local pits and even across the border from East Lothian, filtering into Dalkeith before dawn and congregating in the streets as more and more men arrived. At around one in the afternoon, the town cleared as an estimated four hundred miners filtered into the Freemasons Hall, took their positions and locked the door.

Apprehensive of trouble, and always with the continued menace of the Chartists on the horizon, the Duke of Buccleuch and Sir John Hope called up the military. When the colliers emerged from the hall, a company of the 53rd Foot faced them. The redcoats had force marched from Edinburgh and now stood at attention, Brown Bess muskets held ready, bayonets in scabbards at their waist, scarlet uniforms brilliant in the autumn sun.

With the military lined up opposite the hall, the Duke of Buccleuch, together with his chamberlain, Mr Moncrieff, marched to the door, backed up by twenty newly- recruited Special Constables. At first, the colliers refused to allow the Duke into what was a private meeting, but eventually, they opened the doors. However, the Duke did not enter alone; as soon as the door opened, most of the Specials barged in, all blue uniforms and massive staffs. In the stunned silence, Moncrieff read out a warrant for the arrest of several miners whom the authorities wanted for offences from rioting to intimidation of those men who did not agree with the strike. With the names announced, the chamberlain asked for the men themselves to step forward and give themselves up. Not surprisingly, nobody accepted his kind invitation.

The Duke and his police escort left the building and waited outside. After another half-hour, the meeting ended, and the colliers filed into the street. The police recognised three of the men they wanted and grabbed them, slipping on the handcuffs right away. They arrested a fourth man on the Dalkeith streets later. Two of the men detained outside the hall, Thomas and McLellan, were released the following Tuesday, with Robert and David Gordon, whom the police arrested in their own home at Old Craighall, set free the same day.

Although the newspapers reported that the miners carried bludgeons, there was no trouble in Dalkeith. Presumably, the press was exaggerating, or the reporters honestly mistook walking sticks for offensive weapons. Most of the military were sent back to Edinburgh, with only a score or so patrolling the streets. As the evening wore on, the miners drifted back to their homes. By that stage, the strikers were desperate. They had been idle for seven weeks, any credit they had at local shops was exhausted, they had sold all that could be sold of their possessions so many, if not most were only eating what they could steal from the local fields, much to the anger of the farmers. For example, William Robertson was given fourteen days in jail for taking potatoes from a pit near New Craighall. The authorities released him the very next day while James Morgan of Old Craighall was given forty days for stealing fowls at Fisherrow.

However, some of the idle colliers sunk to crimes a lot worse than mere petty theft. On Thursday 15th September, three colliers from Old Craighall, James Jamieson, James McLellan and James Workings grabbed and raped Mrs Inglis as she was gleaning what she could find in a field of stubble at Monktonhall farm. Her husband was away from home, searching for work. Mrs Inglis told her neighbours, and somebody informed Constable Simpson of Musselburgh. The constable whistled up a second policeman, and the two of them arrested all three rapists.

As October began, the employers began to pay off the strikers for "deserting their service" by not turning up for work. Colliers at West Bugans at Newbattle were amongst the first to be fired, with the men also losing their homes. The mine owners claimed that the colliers were not yearly tenants; they were labourers who occupied the houses only as long as they worked at West Bugans. To add injury to persecution, the sheriff-substitute, Sheriff Tait, ordered that the evicted and unemployed men should also pay the costs incurred when they tried to defend themselves in court. Sheriff Riddell signed an order for another twenty-six evictions at Elphinstone.

On Monday 10th October, the colliers had a further meeting near the Gallowshall Toll, which stood in Eskbank. The local policeman he sensibly walked away when the miners quietly advised him that it might be better if he was elsewhere. By then the resolution of the Coal Masters was splitting. When Sir John Hope and Mr Stenhouse had agreed to raise the miners' pay from a halfpenny for every tub of coal they filled to a penny, the majority of their colliers returned to work. Other Coal Masters agreed among themselves to hold out against the miners for another two weeks at least, in other words, to try and starve the colliers into submission. In the meantime, the colliers scrabbled for food so they could continue the struggle.

There was a slight mist on the morning of the 24th September 1842. Constables Falconer and Macpherson of the County Police had been on patrol all night and were tired and stiff, hoping for a quiet finish to their shift so they could get home. They walked along the ridge from the village of Gorebridge to Gowkshill Farm, where a slight breeze thinned the mist. Falkner checked his watch, saw it was about half-past two in the morning, and stopped as he heard the distinct murmur of voices.

"I heard it too," Macpherson said.

The police loosened their truncheons and shone their bull's-eye lanterns, wondering who was out at this time of night. Their first thought would be poachers, but then they saw a shadowy figure emerge from a potato field to the side of the farm. Although the mist deflected the beam of their lanterns, they could see it was a grown man with a sack on his back. The first man was followed by a second, and then a third and a fourth. The men kept coming until the police counted fourteen men leaving the field, each with a bulging sack across his shoulders.

Brave men, the constables moved into action, and they arrested the final two of the potato-thieves. There was a moment of confusion, the prisoners yelled for help, and the other men dropped their bags and scrambled back. Within seconds, both police had been knocked down, Macpherson's prisoner was running free, and there was a knot of desperate men around Falconer. Despite the repeated blows and kicks, he was stubborn and slipped handcuffs around his prisoner's wrists. Still under attack, the police battled through the crowd and dragged their struggling prisoner to Gowkshill farmhouse, where Mr Proudfoot the farmer opened the door, ushered them in and hastily closed up, drawing a bolt to keep things secure. The other potato-thieves lifted their spoil and piled through the door of a nearby cottage.

No doubt shaken, the police had no intention of relinquishing their prisoner, so while Macpherson remained in the farmhouse with the potato thief, Falconer took on the dangerous job of rounding up the men who had run. In any community, there are those willing to aid the police and those to whom the police are the enemy. In 1842, with the Midlothian colliers involved in the General Strike, the demarcation lines were strictly drawn.

Falconer knew it would be stupid to barge alone into a cottage containing a dozen desperate men, so he whistled up a reluctant farm servant, asked him to keep an eye on things and marched to the local farms to gather more reinforcements. With a gang of hungry colliers on the prowl, nobody's fields were safe, so the farmers joined in with the police. With two or three men at his back, Falconer returned to the cottage where he had left his sentry, to find the man vanished and in his place a mob of around two hundred colliers together with their wives and sisters, all looking decidedly hostile. Although it was the men who carried weapons, it was a woman who shouted out:

"Here is the police! Kill him!"

The instant the words were said, several colliers rushed forward, swinging long lengths of stick and shouting abuse. Falconer's supporters seem to have been conspicuous by their absence as the colliers knocked the policeman to the ground. Already bleeding from two wounds on his forehead and a deep cut on his chin, Falconer struggled to his feet. He found that the colliers had formed a ring around him; in the half-light of early morning, he saw predatory faces; he heard the sound of angry, rough voices; women shrieking and men cursing. Falconer knew he was alone and unpopular amongst people with no cause to love a representative of the authorities.

Falconer lunged to escape, just as one of the women threw a massive stone that caught him full in the chest. He was lucky that his uniform great-coat took part of the force of the blow, but he was still knocked to the ground for the third time that morning, and this time the mob closed, boots hammering at him. He crawled away, rose to his feet and fled, pursued by the hoots of the colliers. He made it as far as the next-door field before he fell again and lay for some time before he was able to stagger to Gorebridge, where Dr Symington dressed his wounds, cuts and abrasions. After that, the doctor judged that he was not fit to walk and ordered him to a nearby cottage to recover.

While Falconer was braving the colliers, Macpherson was also busy. As soon as the mob realised that one of their number was held a prisoner in Gowkshill Farm, they gathered outside, booted down the door and rushed in. Macpherson pulled his truncheon and moved to stop them but a howling horde of collier women and men rushed at him, somebody smashed him over the head with the shaft of a pick-axe, and he slumped senseless on the floor. The women were most forward in hustling the prisoner away, although there are no details of how they removed or cut away his handcuffs.

Rounds one and two to the colliers, but with the whole country in an uproar and seemingly in danger of significant civil disruption, the authorities knew they could not allow matters to rest like that. When the police superintendent heard what had happened, he sent a sergeant and several constables to Gowkshill to find and arrest the rioters. It was a brave, but a forlorn attempt. By the time the handful of police arrived, around four hundred colliers were waiting.

Wherever the police went, a hostile crowd of colliers surrounded them; desperate men who were idle, angry and determined. The police asked questions, looking for signs of guilt as the colliers refused to co-operate in any way. The police were getting nowhere and no doubt the frustration was growing, so they would welcome the advice of Mr McGilvray, the factor of the Marquis of Lothian who owned the collieries. McGilvray said that, given the numbers of men and women involved, the police could do nothing, and it would be better if they instead gave a full report to the sheriff.

Faced with an increasingly hostile crowd, the police sergeant agreed and withdrew. Sheriff Spiers would have been well aware of the situation, and as soon as the mine-owners officially notified him, he requested military help to back up the over-stretched blue line. Mounted troops had proven themselves as the most effective weapon to end civil disturbance and accordingly twenty-five Enniskillen Dragoons clattered out of Piershill Barracks in Edinburgh and took the road south to Midlothian. They rendezvoused with Sheriff Spiers while Mr List, the superintendent of Police, gathered together as many constables as he could and headed to the tiny settlement of Gowkshill.

With the dragoons as grim support, the police searched through the houses for those men and women who had helped rescue the two prisoners. Naturally, the colliers were not co-operative. They had long before spirited away the missing men. Even with the dragoons, the police found nothing. Sometime after nine at night, the Enniskillens rattled back to barracks, and the police were alone.

There was an uneasy peace that night as the police patrolled, hoping that nothing happened, while the colliers continued the strike, desperate for better days. And then the trouble erupted again, and for the same reason. The police saw a lone miner digging potatoes from the edge of a field and immediately plunged in to arrest him. Perhaps they had been waiting for a chance for revenge, or they were determined to show that legal authority was still in charge in Edinburghshire, but they dragged away their man in triumph.

What happened next was predictable. The colliers gathered again and rescued the prisoner, with two of the police injured in the inevitable confrontation. This time the police did not take any chances. They had the names and addresses of four men who had been involved in this later rescue but, rather than go alone and risk a further riot, Sheriff Spiers issued arrest warrants for each man.

Learning from past mistakes, the police came in with full force. A company of the 53rd Foot marched to Old Craighall and stood by with their muskets, ball ammunition and bayonets while Sheriff Spiers joined the Duke of Buccleuch, Lord Lieutenant of the county, Superintendent List and a substantial body of police in journeying to Gowkshill. Faced with such an august body of men backed by lethal force, the recalcitrant colliers reluctantly gave up four of their own for trial and lengthy sentences.

That strike, like so many others, eventually petered out, defeated by starvation and lack of funds. The fight, however, continued. The Chartists flared into prominence in 1848 with a massive petition for electoral reform, which the government duly ignored, but their legacy lived on, and possibly still does live on in the Labour party and the present electoral system. The part played by Midlothian miners has been forgotten. Gowkshill remains, now a small local authority housing estate with the farm as a livery stable. It is unlikely that many people know of its part in history back in the 1840s.

Chapter 4

THE KILLING AT THE COAL PIT

Naturally, in an environment where many men worked in hard physical labour and in total reliance on each other, close bonds were formed, but there could also be personality friction and differences of opinion. Most often, these differences resulted in only high words that faded away and were forgotten in the overall drama of life. At other times there were more tragic results.

One of the latter occurred on the morning of Saturday the 18th of June 1853 at a pit at the Cowden Cleugh (otherwise Cowden Cleuch) coal mine, a mile or so to the east of Dalkeith. The Duke of Buccleuch was the owner of the mine, but he would hardly be aware of its existence, mainly because at that period the mine had been out of operation for many years. In May 1853, Henry Cadell of Thornybank, Dalkeith, who managed all of the Duke's mines, had decided to reopen the pit. Cadell's decision meant that years of accumulated rubbish had to be cleaned out before men could be again sent down to mine the coal. The pit was locally known as Poole's Hole after a man named Poole who committed suicide in the early years of the century, and it was a place generally avoided. However, when Cadell passed the word that he intended to clear it, John McCallum agreed to accept the work at eight shillings a fathom, with a fathom being six feet. He hired two men to do the actual labouring work: John Donohue, an Irishman who lived at Fisherrow, by Musselburgh, and William Corner.

McCallum ensured that the windlass at the head of the shaft was in working order and ordered a new rope of 54 yarns. Ropes were vital to the operation of the pits: they supported the weight of the coal that toiling workers raised from the bottom in large buckets, and also of the men as they were lowered to the bottom of the pit to begin working at the coal seam. A rope of 54 yarns was one of the best. Such a cable should last at least a year and perhaps as long as eighteen months before wear and strain weakened it until it was no longer safe. A mining expert believed that if even two yarns were intact, a good rope should be capable of supporting the weight of a man. The windlass was hand operated with two lines attached to a cylinder and a handle at each end, so ideally two miners could work it while the third was underground toiling away at the actual digging. One rope wound up as the other unwound, and the man beneath ground put the spoil in a bucket, so one full bucket was taken up at the same time as the surface workers lowered the next, empty, bucket to him. The man at the bottom of the pit was lowered and raised by the same procedure, balancing on the bucket as the men at the top worked the windlass.

McCallum, as the contractor, was in charge of the clearing operations and always remained above ground while John Donaghue and Corner took turns at working down below.

The work was laborious, digging out the accumulated rubbish, so progress was not as fast as McCallum had hoped. As the labourers dug deeper into the pit, the work grew ever more difficult, and McCallum and Corner decided that they were not being paid enough. In the middle of May, McCallum approached Thomas Stewart, the Dalkeith mine overseer, and tried to raise the contract price for sinking the pit. He said they had reached fifteen fathoms and the work was becoming harder. Stewart agreed to raise the price to ten shillings for every fathom they dug and thought that was the end of the matter, but on about the 9th of June, McCallum returned and asked for another raise. This time Stewart turned him down, saying "you have not been getting on so rapidly with your work as you might have done." The price remained at ten shillings a fathom, and the work grew progressively more arduous and therefore slower.

Friday the 17th of June was the Dalkeith sacramental fast, and the collieries stopped work. At about half-past six on Saturday morning, McCallum ran to Stewart in a very agitated state. McCallum blurted out that a man had been killed in Poole's Hole. Stewart tried to calm him down and asked how the accident had occurred, but McCallum appeared too agitated to give a coherent answer, although he did gabble something about somebody cutting the rope. McCallum also said he had been so tired that he had been in bed all Friday and had not been at Poole's Hole since Thursday. Without giving any more details, McCallum said he would run to town and fetch a doctor.

As soon as McCallum had gone, Stewart told Cadell what had happened and then hurried along to Poole's Hole. By the time he arrived, busy hands had taken the body out of the pit. It seemed that before he came to Stewart, McCallum had told the workers in the nearby Cowden Cleuch quarry, and a group of quarrymen had rushed over to the pit. They descended the eighteen fathoms, about 108 feet, and found Donaghue severely injured, with both his legs smashed, a broken spine and other injuries. Not surprisingly, he died very soon after and the quarrymen managed to get his body up to the surface.

Stewart examined the rope: McCallum was right. Somebody had cut into it. He had been in the mining business long enough to know that the cable had not parted through strain with overuse; instead, all except three or four yarns had been sliced through with a very sharp blade. Stewart thought that Donaghue had fallen about fifty feet, judging by the damage to the rope.

Stewart saw Corner among the crowd that gathered around Donaghue's broken body and asked him if he had been at the pit on the previous day. Corner shook his head emphatically; he had not been there. As Stewart questioned Corner, McCallum arrived at the pit, still very excited; he said that he should go and tell Mrs Donaghue that her husband was dead. Cadell thought that was a good idea and gave him a pound for the new widow, presumably to compensate for the loss of her husband. However, one of the assembled quarrymen thought that McCallum was too overwrought and suggested that somebody calmer should break the news.

Donald McDonald was one of the quarrymen who had helped raise Donaghue's body. His memory of what had occurred was slightly different from McCallum's. McDonald said that when they reached the mine, McCallum had claimed he was "so much agitated" that he could not go down the pit, and asked McDonald to go instead. McDonald thought that a bit strange; he was also curious why Corner made no move to go and help his colleague until he heard that others were going down. It was even more interesting that McCallum said that some colliers from another pit had been arguing with Donaghue over religion and had cut the rope.

Rather than discuss the reason for Donaghue's fall, McDonald was more concerned with the results. He thought he heard a man 'sprawling about' at the bottom of the pit and who "seemed as if choking in water." Either through coercion or because he was genuinely concerned, Corner was first down the pit, with McDonald next. By the time McDonald reached him, Donaghue had died. Together, McDonald and Corner had put Donaghue's body in the bucket and signalled for the men above to haul it to the surface.

As they waited in the gloom for the bucket to come back down to get them out, McDonald asked Corner if he had cut the rope.

"No," Corner replied distinctly, "but for the love of God let me up this pit and I'll never come down again."

"Where's your knife?" McDonald asked as strong hands removed Donaghue's body from the bucket. There would be a moment's tension as he spoke to a possible murderer.

"For the love of God never mention that," Corner sounded shaken by the questioning. "I never had a knife since I came to the work."

As they took Donaghue's body to Thornybank, they stopped to share half a mutchkin of whisky "to take off the shaking" as McDonald put it.

With Donaghue laid safely away, Corner and a quarryman named James Anderson walked to Fisherrow to break the news to Donaghue's wife, Mary Ann. Perhaps because of the time they had spent taking the body to Thornybank, or maybe just because news spreads fast in small communities, Mrs Donaghue already knew what had happened. Rather than mourn, as soon as Corner entered her house at around ten in the morning, she launched a full-frontal verbal assault on him, blaming him for her husband's murder.

When Anderson told her that he thought that somebody had taken either a pick or an axe to the rope, Mary Donaghue said: "I blame the man who worked with him."

Anderson gestured to Corner. "This is the man," he said, possibly hoping that Mary Donaghue was mistaken or merely upset. Instead, she faced Corner directly and said:

"Then you are the man that murdered my husband, and no other."

Corner lowered his voice to what Mary Donaghue later described as "so deadly a tone that you would have thought it was coming out of the earth."

"Mistress," Corner said, "if I injured your husband do you think I would come here? No, God forbid."

As Corner denied any involvement, Donaghue's mother-in-law joined in, supporting her daughter.

Mary Donaghue had her reasons for blaming Corner. She knew that her husband had been working with McCallum and Corner at Poole's Hole for over a month, and he had often come home with some disturbing stories. On at least two occasions, Donaghue had been working at the bottom of the pit when great stones had come hurtling down from above. One, weighing about two pounds, had sliced open his right shoulder, and on Thursday before he died, a rock that he estimated weighed at least five pounds had fallen or had been thrown at him. He had only escaped by hugging the side of the mine.

Although on both these occasions Corner and McCallum had been on top of the pit, Mary Ann had known McCallum for some time and trusted him. She neither knew nor trusted Corner, while her husband said he "never had any quarrel" with the contractor.

Even with his suspicions about Corner, Donaghue had not intended leaving the job: work was work. When Mary Donaghue again accused Corner, he said "I will pull you up another day for it."

It was evident that they could do no good in that house, so Corner and Anderson returned to Dalkeith, with Corner so upset that he trembled and occasionally had to sit by the roadside to collect his strength. However, he did not allow the matter to rest there and visited the Donaghues' house a few times that same morning with protestations of innocence.

"You are the man," Mary Donaghue repeated each time.

Already distraught over the death of her husband, Mary Donaghue must have been driven to distraction by the repeated visits of his work colleagues, for McCallum also came to see her. He used different tactics. Playing on their shared Irish nationality, he would place his right arm on her shoulder; take hold of her hand and say:

"Mary Ann, do not blame me, for we are sacred of the murder; the plot was laid for me and him, as we are Irish."

Mrs Donaghue, however, was not as naïve as McCallum hoped. "Don't say so, John," she responded. "The plot could not be laid for you, for you never went down." She reminded McCallum that she knew he only went below ground once, and that was "for your own pleasure" and not to work, and added that nobody would know what nationality her husband was for he had a Scottish accent.

Mary Ann was very open with McCallum. She told him that her husband had gone to work at four in the morning of the day he died. She also said that she had asked Donaghue if he had told anybody that he intended to work that day. He had not replied directly to that, but according to Mary Ann, he had said that his colleagues "had a spite against him."

When McCallum heard those words, he turned the conversation to the colliers of Cowdenfoot and claimed that they had cut the rope with a pick or an axe. At the same time, he asked to see Mary Ann's children, of whom he seemed genuinely fond. At that point, McCallum said that when Donaghue's body was returned to her, the two would have a "long talk."

Mary Ann refused to follow that trend and instead repeated her accusation of Corner, who was in the house at the time.

McCallum defended his compatriot. Holding up his hand, he said that Corner "is as sacred of the murder as I am," and said "believe me, Mary Ann; we are innocent." He repeated that they were all friends and had not quarrelled, so there was no reason for murder.

Mary Ann must have asked what had happened on her husband's last day. McCallum told her that immediately Donaghue arrived at the pit, he had sent him to the store. Donaghue had taken so long that McCallum and Corner had gone to make sure he was all right. Unable to locate him, McCallum and Corner had returned to the pit. They were there about twenty minutes before Donaghue arrived and he had stepped into the basket – the bucket – to be lowered to the bottom. "God have mercy on me," Donaghue said, and then the bucket was lowered, the rope snapped, and he plunged down into the darkness beneath.

On the following day, Sunday, the quarryman McDonald again met Corner and, still suspicious, asked him: "Willie, have you no put the man away amongst yoursels?"

Corner shook his head violently. "God forbid that I would ever do anything of the kind."

McDonald, who was obviously a shrewd, direct man, then asked Corner why he had denied being at the pit on Friday.

Corner was unhappy at being put on the spot. He reluctantly agreed that he had been at the workings and said he "did not recollect" why he had thought otherwise.

The authorities also suspected Corner and McCallum. After all, they were with Donaghue when he died and had direct access to the cut rope. Sergeant Alexander Reid of the County Police interviewed both men on the evening of Saturday the 18th of June, the same day that Donohue died. Immediately the police arrested them, both men denied that they had been at the pit or indeed outside of Dalkeith between the Thursday night and Saturday morning. When Sergeant Reid returned from taking them to Calton Jail, he found a razor amongst Corner's possessions. The blade was dulled with use and smeared with the same type of tar that coated the cut rope.

The trial was on Friday the 22nd of July, with McCallum and Corner charged with murder "in having conspired to kill or to do serious bodily injury to John Donaghue, labourer." The Lord Justice General, together with Lords Anderson and Cowan sat on the bench, be-wigged and stern as they presided over the fifteen men of the jury who would decide the life or death of the two accused. McCallum and Corner both pleaded not guilty.

The evidence was almost all circumstantial. Thomas Sharp, a miner from Cowdenfoot, stated that two weeks or so before the death, McCallum had told him the work was progressing slowly. Then there was another miner named William Archibald, who had met McCallum and Corner between Dalkeith and Cowdenfoot on the Thursday before the death. He overheard a snatch of conversation in which Corner said: "I'll do for that bugger someday." As he knew Corner, Archibald thought it safe to ask about whom he was talking, but rather than explain, Corner threatened to give him "a kicking." Sensibly, Archibald decided not to ask any more questions.

A quarryman named James Houston happened to be standing in Moffat's Close, which was where McCallum lived, on the evening of the 17th of June. McCallum and Corner were both there, and Corner said, "mind tomorrow night, John."

A few moments later, McCallum said "mind the morning, Willie." Houston saw both men together at ten on Friday morning - the day McCallum claimed he had spent in bed. Another man named James Hope also saw both men walking toward Poole's Hole on Friday morning. McCallum told him they were making sure there were no "mischievous laddies" there. During the same conversation, Corner informed Hope that a stone had recently fallen on "the Irishman," who had "roared as if he had been killed." Corner said that he had gone down the pit to ensure Donaghue was all right and found there was nothing wrong with him. McCallum also said that the job paid "fine."

Other people also saw McCallum and Corner together that day: Margaret More saw both walking toward Poole's Pit in their working clothes, while George Dickson spoke to them in the afternoon as they walked toward Dalkeith. Again, McCallum said that they had been checking the pit to make sure there were "no laddies working mischief."

Finally, there was Ann Drummond, who shared the same house as Corner. She said that he left the house about eleven in the morning of Friday the 17th of June, and came back about two in the afternoon. He went to bed about eight, which makes sense if he was up early to start work, but for some reason he said:

"Ann, I'm going to bed, but God knows how I am to sleep."

That statement haunted Ann, who said it was "very strange of him to say that."

When the police sifted through all the vague evidence of the witnesses, they thought that it proved only that Corner and McCallum were at the pit on Friday when both had said they were not. After that, both men's statements were read out. McCallum claimed that on Friday 17th, Corner had said he would be "revenged on that mate of yours," meaning John Donaghue. McCallum asked why, and Corner replied, "for everything and because I do not like him." McCallum added that it was not the first time that Corner had said he would "do for him." He put that down to jealousy as he thought Donaghue was the better worker of the two.

Naturally, Corner gave a different story. He stated that McCallum borrowed his razor to cut the rope. The idea was to cause an accident that injured Donaghue so either their wages would rise, or the contract would be cancelled. However, he did not think McCallum intended killing Donaghue.

Both the Solicitor General and the Lord Justice General pointed out that Corner had admitted some guilt, while there was no hard evidence against McCallum. The Lord Justice General added that he could not treat the declaration of one prisoner as evidence against another.

The facts were very confused, and the motive seemed unclear. The prosecution tried to prove that McCallum and Corner had thought their payment for re-opening the shaft was too little for the work involved, and if Donaghue were injured or killed, the contract would be cancelled. There was also a slight possibility that McCallum had intentions that were more than friendly to Donaghue's widow, but the court did not pursue that aspect of the case.

The jury agreed found both men guilty of culpable homicide. The Lord Justice-General sentenced them to ten years transportation. That seems to have been a bit of a compromise as if the judges believed they had been guilty of murder but could not prove it. The mystery was never conclusively solved.

Chapter 5

EARLY POLICING IN MIDLOTHIAN

Overshadowed by the capital, Midlothian's people may think that police and criminal history has neglected the county. They have a point, as nobody has written extensively about either. However, the birth and early years of the Midlothian, Edinburghshire, or simply the County police has its interest separate from, yet geographically attached to, that of the city of Edinburgh.

Scotland had seen the first municipal police force in Great Britain with the advent of the Glasgow Police in 1800. Edinburgh followed soon after, in 1804, with Dundee and Aberdeen adding their forces in the 1820s so that by the middle of the decade, Scotland's four main urban centres were all covered. In 1829 Robert Peel's Metropolitan Police Force arrived with great fanfare, and after that, there was a demand for more organised policing throughout the rural as well as urban districts of Britain.

Simultaneous with the desire for reform in law enforcement, was concern about the treatment of prisoners. With the death penalty becoming less used and various colonies becoming reluctant to absorb Britain's unwanted criminals, the use of prisons as places of long-term incarceration became more critical. Until then, Scotland's prisons were run by local burghs and counties; they were haphazard, unsanitary and often insecure. The government appointed Frederick Hill as Scotland's first inspector of prisons, and his annual reports make interesting reading about the state of crime and criminality in Scotland on the advent of county police forces.

In December 1837, Hill's report highlighted an overall increase in crime throughout Scotland, which people blamed on a trade depression. There were other comments of particular interest to Midlothian, such as "of all offences now common in Scotland, those arising out of combinations of workmen are by far the most formidable." At that time working men and women were only beginning to come together to form "combinations" to fight the evils under which they laboured. Some of these combinations sought such things as better working conditions or a living wage, but there were occasions when those opposed to the combinations had a rough time. Violence on both sides was not uncommon, and the widespread miners' strike was only a few years in the future.

However, Hill also believed that "offences now committed are of a much milder character than those that were perpetrated thirty or forty years ago and the total amount of crime when compared to the extent of population has much decreased." He believed that crime could be specific to a particular occupation; for instance, coal carters were men with criminal tendencies and prone to theft, while "wandering tinkers... almost synonymous with theft." Colliers and fishermen, however, were considered honest, although they drank too much and then committed breaches of the peace and assaults. Hill put the primary cause of crime as drunkenness with the root of that as: "the want of a cultivated taste for other than mere sensual gratification."

His beliefs about wandering tinkers and other travellers were mirrored by Midlothian's first chief constable when he took over only three years later. Edinburgh had long had an issue with beggars, so a Society for the Suppression of Begging was created there in 1813, with over six hundred professional beggars arrested in the following year.

In 1837, there were lock-up houses (primitive jails) in Dalkeith, Lasswade and Penicuik, with those at Dalkeith and Penicuik also used for short terms of imprisonment. Hill recommended that the council should build new prisons at Penicuik and Dalkeith. There were also eight police cells for miscreants plus a single room for vagrants in the County Hall. The jail at Penicuik was a single cell, eight feet square and twelve feet high, on the ground floor of a church tower in the "present churchyard on one side of the village;" presumably, this was St Mungo's church.

Hill also said that significant crimes such as murder, highway robbery and "other heinous offences" were infrequent in Midlothian. However, there were sufficient to case travellers to be wary. Housebreaking with violence was unknown, although stealing from domestic premises without violence was common while thefts of potatoes, turnips or poultry, as well as petty assaults, were widespread. Boys between eight and eighteen committed many of the minor thefts. It is possible that a mixture of boredom, hunger and under-employment motivated such crimes, or perhaps the miscreants were merely young men pushing the boundaries to see how much they could get away with: Youth does not change much through time. Again, echoing later observers, Hill said that most of the offenders drink heavily, have no regular employment and are under-educated, with parents of "bad character."

On the other hand, Hill also thought that although the sheriff officers were "respectable and efficient," the county needed an 'organised and efficient' police force.

Penicuik had the occasional serious crime but mostly only drunken squabbles and petty thefts. There were few known criminals, and the worst was a handful of regular poachers, plus a few "suspicious characters." Recent crimes included a man who shot a policeman in the early 1830s and a tragic murder in Silverburn, while two years back, in 1835, the authorities had ejected a band of ten tinkers that had been causing trouble. They moved to Selkirkshire and then to Linlithgowshire, where the authorities arrested a few. Overall, Hill thought that even drunkenness was decreasing in the Penicuik area.

Lasswade prison was another that was in a poor state. It was situated in the tower of an old church within the graveyard, with two cells on the ground floor and one on the floor above. The prison officer was an unpaid constable who was also the local blacksmith; he was thought of as an intelligent and respectable man and volunteered for the common good. Hill believed that there was more crime in Lasswade than in Penicuik, with many thefts and assaults. The offenders were slightly older, aged twelve to twenty-four but again had drunken habits and lacked education. Most of the bad characters were from outside the village and included colliers from Loanhead.

The county town, Dalkeith, with a population of 5500, had a prison of two rooms and one cell in the same building as the Justice of the Peace court. There were about thirty prisoners a year, mainly for drunkenness, and most stayed a single night, so it was hardly a crime-ridden town. The sheriff officer in charge was paid £5 a year; he was efficient and, over the previous few years, had reduced crime, although there was still petty theft and drunken brawling. People believed that most crimes were committed by about half a dozen men in their late teens and twenties who did not hesitate to steal or assault and, as usual, there was a larger group of younger boys who admired them and hoped to emulate their bad example. Added to the habitual criminals were a dozen part-time prostitutes, the only Midlothian ladies of the street that Hill mentioned. Like many of their kind at that period, the Dalkeith prostitutes were prone to stealing when they could. Once again, the parents of the young offenders were also dissolute and immoral characters, while some were colliers from outside the town. According to Hill, Midlothian's sheriff officers were often called away on other business and could not attend all the crime, increasing the need for a uniformed police force.

Midlothian certainly was not crime-free in the days before a professional police force. For example, in the late winter of 1800, a man named Peter Anderson broke into a house and shop in Dalkeith. Anderson came through a window, saw a chest of drawers, cracked open the lock and stole twelve shillings (60 pence in today's money) in silver coins. He confessed at his trial, possibly hoping his quick admittance would turn the judge to the mercy that the jury recommended. Instead, the Lord Justice Clerk sentenced him to be hanged. However, his sentence was later reduced to imprisonment "during his Majesty's pleasure."

The authorities never treated theft that involved housebreaking lightly. In 1835 there was a spate of house and shop breaking in southern Edinburgh and Midlothian, with thieves targeting Dalkeith and Loanhead. There was a case on a snowy night in March 1838, when two thieves forced open the door of the stables at Braidwood farm at Penicuik. Although four farm workers were sleeping in the stables, the thieves took their time. They checked the chests first, and as they were locked, they searched for the keys. No keys were hanging up, so the thieves looked around and dexterously slid a bunch free from under the pillow of one of the sleeping workers.

Slowly and stealthily the thieves opened the chests and stole two silver watches, a plaid, some silver coins and a pair of shoes. They slipped away as quietly as they had arrived and no doubt thought they had got away free. However, when the farm servants woke the next morning, they realised that somebody had robbed them. They cast around for culprits, noticed two sets of footprints in the snow heading toward Edinburgh and notified the authorities.

The Edinburgh police were quick off the mark and followed their usual procedure of checking the pawn shops and comparing anything handed in with the list of stolen property. As a pair of policemen entered one pawn shop, they saw two women in the act of handing in the two stolen silver watches. The officers made a rapid arrest, which saw the women jailed, and the farm workers get their property back. That was undoubtedly an excellent result for the police.

Sometimes the amounts involved seem very trivial when compared to the figures that are in use today, but one must always remember that the vast majority of people in Scotland lived on the edge of poverty. An honest artisan might have wages of one pound a week while women could take home half that if she was lucky. Servants might earn as little as five pounds a year, plus board and keep, so the theft of a few shillings could mean the difference between comfort and hunger, or paying the rent or being evicted.

However, it was not a spate of such thefts that pressurised the government, but something deemed much more sinister. In 1839, the Chartists alarmed the establishment with demands for electoral reform, and when some activists proved capable of using physical force to back their demands, the government was edged toward the acceptance of rural police forces to help keep this new threat, as well as crime, at bay.

In 1840 the Midlothian, or Edinburghshire, police force was formed with Alfred John List as the Chief Constable, or Superintendent as he was more often known. Under his guidance, the Midlothian or "County" constabulary initially supported the landed gentry at the expense of the most outcast of society, the landless, rootless travelling folk, both official wanderers and those who were merely searching for something or somewhere to settle.

List was not a local man. Brought up in London, his mother was Welsh, and his father was a Hungarian who ran a London sugar refinery. It was hardly the sort of background one would associate with a Midlothian police officer. However, he was a dyed-in-the-wool law enforcer who joined Robert Peel's fledgling Metropolitan police in September 1829 and in April the following year was promoted to inspector. In 1832, following a series of disturbances and fire-raisings, Haddingtonshire – East Lothian – made him their first police Superintendent. He used the metropolitan system of dividing the county into districts, each with a full-time constable aided by part-timers, used his men to gather information, patrol known criminal haunts and watch those people who already had a criminal record. In particular, the new police were keen to move the travelling gypsies and Irish out of the county and protect the respectable. Frederick Hill would have approved.

Midlothian certainly had a history of problems with what people then termed vagabonds. In April 1741, a gang of "tinkers, gypsies, sorners and vagabonds, many of them armed" according to the *Caledonian Mercury*, infested the county, annoying the local population by stealing what they could and frightening the occupants of isolated cottages and farmhouses. They made their base in and around Carrington, south of Dalkeith, and specialised in robbing doocots.

The authorities managed to grab that particular gang, locked them in the stocks in Dalkeith Tolbooth, slammed shut the cell door and thought they had done an excellent job. However, the gypsies had other ideas. They somehow released themselves from the stocks first and then broke free from the jail. Cursing their luck, the authorities, joined by some locals, searched for the escapees, including one "of a very black complexion, high and thin aged about 35", named Thomas Tait or Thomas Stewart. He "wore a white periwig and black coat, five foot 6 or 8 inches. The other is Robert Armstrong, same stature, brown coat and white coarse stockings."

Although the authorities did not catch any of that particular band, they succeeded in scooping up another fifteen "idle vagrants" and thrust them into the Tolbooth instead. One hopes that the jailers had improved the security measures.

Fears of such gypsy or sorner bands erupted periodically, with another gang scaring the settled people of Midlothian in May 1759. That month the parish constables arrested a woman named Mary Macdonald in Dalkeith and sent her into the Edinburgh Tolbooth in case she belonged to the gypsy gang. Sorners and gypsies seemed to specialise in breaking out of prisons, for in 1766, four more of a large band of gypsies tried to escape from the Tolbooth in Edinburgh. As they were busily digging through a wall, a considerable chunk of stone fell, making sufficient noise to alert the guards, who placed them in shackles. The men were later charged with horse stealing and petty theft, while their wives were arrested and jailed in Dalkeith.

It was such criminal gangs that justified country areas such as Midlothian creating their own police force. No simple parish constable or isolated justice of the peace could cope with an armed gang, and the army was not always amenable to being summoned to help the civil power.

To make matters worse, the police in Edinburgh had a habit of moving vagrants on by taking them to the southern boundaries of the city and giving them a hefty metaphorical kick in the pants in the direction of Midlothian. Even in the nineteenth century, when it was unusual to see the larger bands of sorners, rootless and often pauper groups would hover around farmsteads, begging for charity and sometimes stealing what they could. It was a problem that was not confined to Midlothian for in Edwin Chadwick's 1839 report on the Royal Commission on Constabulary forces; List said that all Scotland was "very much infested" with vagrants. However, he also stated that rural Scotland was more law-abiding than rural England and the Scottish police procedure superior. In Scotland, the police gathered evidence and presented it to the procurator fiscal, who decided whether or not to charge, and the police interrogated the suspect before a lawyer was present.

List proclaimed that many of the crimes against property – mainly thefts and criminal damage – were caused by people from the cities and large towns. He believed that an efficient rural police force could alleviate the problem. Vagrants of various types, he claimed, were the other main offenders, by pulling down fences, trespassing, rustling and stealing crops. In his treatise of policing, he said that his police had orders to turn out of the county "vagrants, sturdy beggars and suspicious characters." He wanted the police to jail all beggars and feed them on bread and water. He also advised that the police should recruit constables from outside the area so they were not influenced by local friendship or family ties.

Taking List's advice, in their first week of existence, the Edinburghshire Police shifted over a hundred vagrants beyond the county borders. List's appointment may well have pleased the respectable and the establishment who might have felt threatened by the bands of roving travellers. However, it would not be welcomed by the people he targeted, and the Irish who laboured on the Edinburgh to Glasgow railway line believed that they came into that category. They assembled in Dalkeith, frequenting the public houses with the nearly inevitable result of a riot and more arrests. The new police had either provoked trouble or had proved their worth, depending on the viewpoint of the observer.

When List moved from being the Superintendent of Haddingtonshire to begin his tenure in Edinburghshire, his brother moved into Haddington. Of course, List had crimes other than vagrancy to curtail, mostly drunken assaults and petty theft. One such attack took place at Peter Baxter's public house in Dalkeith on the 27th December 1840, in List's first year. A labourer named Alexander Baxter had been celebrating Christmas a little too liberally but had forgotten that he had to pay for the whisky he was pouring down his throat. When Peter Baxter, the publican, asked for payment, Alexander Baxter made a dive for the door, only for the publican to grab hold of his arm. Alexander retaliated by punching him to the ground. When Peter called for help, John Archibald, Sheriff Officer and Constable James Park intervened and after a titanic struggle that saw Alexander Baxter assault both men, Park and Archibald subdued and arrested him. As Alexander Baxter had previous convictions for assault, the case went to the High Court in February 1841, and the judge sentenced him to seven years transportation.

Life for the police in the early years was rough, for they were unpopular with ordinary people and anybody with a grievance or one drink too many could target them. One of many such cases occurred at Straiton, in January 1857, when a local pub held a raffle and one group of men including James Laing, a banksman from Lasswade, John Laing, coal grieve at Loanhead and a few visitors from Edinburgh disputed the winner with a gamekeeper named George Hay. The whole bunch attacked Hay, and when David Campbell, the New Pentland policeman, intervened to prevent a murder, he too was attacked. The Police Court fined all the attackers a pound.

There were many other assaults. For example, at the High Court, in December 1845, a Loanhead collier named Kenneth Young was given six months for stabbing a fellow collier named George Sneddon and then punching him in the face. Loanhead featured in another case, in May 1846, when two Rosewell colliers, Henry and John Brown, assaulted two Loanhead men, George Brown, a spirit dealer and an iron founder named George Easthope. The court fined them three pounds. No area was free, and there was no telling when an assault could take place. On Saturday 7th July 1866, a carter named William Inglis and his wife were walking home to Bonnyrigg. They had just passed the Bonnyrigg Toll Bar when George Archibald of Newtongrange attacked them for no apparent reason. He punched both to the ground and booted both as they lay helpless, breaking Inglis's jaw, and kicked one of his wife's teeth from her mouth. He was given four months in jail.

These assaults may not have been major crimes to men such as List, but to the victims, each case would be a traumatic event in their lives. Probably even more prevalent was theft.

There has probably been petty theft since the first cavemen saw their cave-neighbours had a nicely shaped club, and nineteenth-century Midlothian was no exception. Some thefts would be hard to understand today, such as when a pair of widows, Catherine Wilson and Ann Mackay, appeared before Dalkeith Sheriff Court, in June 1841, charged with stealing grass from a field outside Dalkeith. Apparently, the Duke of Buccleuch, the owner, was very attached to the grass but it was Constable Duncan Falconer of the County Police who arrested the women. The sheriff gave Ann McKay 30 days and Catherine Wilson 14 days in jail to ponder their sins.

In a rural and semi-rural county such as Midlothian, trespass and poaching was always a problem. The JP or Police Courts often dealt with sorry-looking men who had been caught poaching. For example, in the Dalkeith Justice of the Peace Court in October 1841, four Stobhill colliers, Gardner Davidson and William, David and George Landalls were fined twenty shillings each for "trespass in search of game at Lochquhariot Mains." In the Dalkeith Justice of the Peace court in December 1865, Thomas Wylie, a labourer at the brickworks at Vogrie, was found poaching in Vogrie estate and fined eight shillings. In that same court, two Gorebridge shoemakers, Alexander Wilson and John Henderson were fined five shillings each for poaching on the lands of the North British Railway near Borthwick, and four Whitehill men were fined a pound each for "trespassing in search of game" at Oxenfoord. These are only a few examples, selected at random from a catalogue of poaching offences, some of which had far more severe consequences than a small fine.

There was a sliding scale of punishments in Scotland. A first offence was usually treated leniently, with a small fine or a few days locked away. If a person was caught stealing a second time, he or she would be "by habit and repute" a thief, and the judge would increase the sentence accordingly. For example, in December 1866, a man named Walter McBeth stole a basket from a parked cart in Dalkeith High Street. The vehicle belonged to William Wilson, a Newbattle labourer and his wife owned the basket. She had left it on the cart when she nipped into a baker's shop. However, a little girl had seen McBeth take the basket and told the police he had escaped into Leyden's Close where the police found him a short while later. Because McBeth had four previous convictions, he was sent to the High Court and given seven years penal servitude, which was a substantial sentence.

The Police Courts could award up to sixty days in jail. If the offender ended up at the Sheriff Court, he or she could face up to eighteen months in prison. Any repeated crimes or crimes deemed to be serious involved a visit to the High Court and penalties that included penal servitude, transportation or the hangman's noose. Penal servitude was best avoided, with months or years of solitary confinement and a regime that could see countless hours of pointless hard labour, utter silence, a cell without a mattress and no means of passing the time except for contemplation of one's sins. It was a regime designed to punish the mind as well as the body. Transportation meant years of exile on the far side of the world, with a slender prospect of ever returning home. Until 1868, hangings were in public, with crowds gathering to watch this example of justice. After 1868, culprits were hanged and then buried within the confining walls of the prison, so punishment continued even after death. Prison hangings were sombre affairs, although the other inmates often demonstrated by making as much noise as they could. The prison could toll a bell, or fly the black flag to indicate the terrible event that was happening within.

Today it is recognised that there are many reasons and causes for committing a crime. In the early nineteenth century, many people in authority had more simple ideas. They believed that a weakness of character was behind criminal activity, and were afraid that the spread of industrial towns, with their hordes of mill and factory workers, would see a vast increase in crime.

One offence that was as common then as now is swindling. Today it is more likely to be online, but in the nineteenth century, it was face-to-face. In December 1815, the *Caledonian Mercury* warned people to watch for "a woman of colour" who called herself Matilda Campbell. She was good looking, elegant, about twenty-eight years old and had lived in Dalkeith for some time. According to the newspaper, she tried to con people by claiming she had to get back to her mother and three children in Madras, and used tears to soften unrelenting hearts. However, in reality, she was not a mother and was well known as a "woman of bad character" who toured the Edinburgh and Portobello area looking for money.

Such warnings were not uncommon throughout the century. In July 1829, there was a man touring houses in the Lasswade area, claiming to be the parish schoolmaster of Carrington. He told the householder that there had been a mining accident that killed two men, leaving their widows and twelve children destitute. However, the man was a confidence trickster, and there had been no such accident.

More common in fairs and markets, but often to be met on lonely roads were the thimbleriggers. Their trick was simple: they placed a pea beneath one of three thimbles, shuffled them around and asked some gullible person to guess under which thimble it sat. After a couple of attempts when the customer guessed correctly and thought he or she had the measure of the game, the thimblerigger would suggest they put money on the outcome. If the customer agreed, he or she was doomed. There was one case in late October 1838 when one poor girl gambled all she had on finding the pea and lost. She was in floods of tears when a man came along the road and chased the swindlers away.

Not all women were such hapless victims of crime. In the early afternoon of Friday 17th March 1815, young Margaret Clark said goodbye to her father, George Clark of Ford, and left her house. She was engaged on a private errand, with a small roll of banknotes in her pocket. As she entered a quiet stretch of road, two men in blue jackets came up to her. Both were carrying a bundle, and they looked so menacing that Margaret became very wary.

When one of the men reached out for her, Margaret stepped back and lifted a large stone from the ground. The men did not speak, but while the taller stood in front of her, the other stepped to the side, as if to block her escape. Without hesitation, Margaret threw the stone as hard as she could, catching the taller man on the head, so he dropped to the ground and lay still. Seeing his friend fall, the second man moved toward her, but the formidable Margaret was having none of it. Lifting another rock, she threw it straight at him. Her aim was not quite so good this time, for she missed his head and the stone smacked hard against his shin. The man staggered, with blood running down his leg and onto his shoe, and only then did Margaret run. When she looked back over her shoulder, nobody was following her; with one of her attackers still prone on the ground and the other with a severely injured leg, that is hardly surprising. Margaret never found out who the men were, but if news of her actions spread, such footpads would be less likely to attack a lone woman again.

Other women were the perpetrators, such as Mary Scott and Rosanne Dunning who were given sixty days in jail, in January 1844, for pretending to tell fortunes in Dalkeith High Street. There were always others who may, or may not, have been aware that they were involved in a crime. Mary Wighton was one of these when, in January 1854, she married Hugh Dunn, who was already married to Ann Bailie. Luckily it was Hugh who was convicted of bigamy at the High Court, in January 1855, while Mary only had the sadness that she was not married, or perhaps the relief of knowing she was not tied forever to a man who had proved deceitful. Hugh had fifteen months in jail to wonder about his duo of wives.

Some crimes sound very familiar, although it may be difficult to imagine that in November 1843, two rival stagecoaches driving from Edinburgh to Peebles kept up a tremendous race as far as Penicuik. As they neared the village, the lead horse in one of the coaches fell stone dead on the road, so the coach slewed to one side and came to a halt. There was relief from the passengers, who had been terrified at the terrible speed of the coach. Such "furious driving" was not unusual, and in March 1848, three farm servants were fined a pound apiece, with the option of twenty days in jail for "furious driving" of a farm cart on their return from Dalkeith market. One wonders what the result of a breathalyser would have been!

Another crime that townsfolk did not have to worry about was sheep stealing. In November 1818, James Wilkie a flesher (butcher) of Lasswade, was caught stealing three sheep from the estate of Lord Viscount Melville. The sheep belonged to John Plummer of Dalkeith, a rival flesher so presumably Wilkie had intended to slaughter the sheep for his shop. Instead, he attended the High Court the following January and the judge sentenced him to fourteen years transportation. To end the list of rural crimes, in August 1847 Hamilton Borthwick and Henry Dobson, a brewer and labourer respectively, broke into the Duke of Buccleuch's Sheriffhall doocot by Dalkeith and stole seventy pigeons. Taking the birds to Edinburgh, they sold the lot to a spirit dealer-cum- carrier-pigeon- dealer in Edinburgh's Cowgate and returned home. The spirit dealer sold some of the birds to a man in Dalry, where a group of sportsmen used them as targets at a shooting match. In the meantime, the county police traced the thieves, who gave up the name of the spirit dealer.

When the police raided his home, they found too many birds to identify the duke's property. With surprising ingenuity, the police tied ribbons to the legs of some birds, took them to Samson's Ribs in Edinburgh's Queen's Park and set them free. When many pigeons flew the five miles to Sheriffhall doocot, the police had proved their provenance.

The two thieves, Borthwick and Dobson, were given 18 months and six months, respectively.

In May 1843, the Police Board Committee meeting stated that "after the experience of three years the committee are convinced of the benefits of the rural police in the prevention of crime and the preservation of the peace." In that period Superintendent List said, there had been 860 summary convictions as compared to 355 in the three years before the police were founded. List did not think that crime had increased, but his new police were more efficient in catching lawbreakers. He added that as many crimes were committed "under the cloud of night," in the previous winter, he arranged a night duty route within a circle of ten miles from Edinburgh and had the roads patrolled by constables in pairs. Their presence reduced thefts, and they also detected many crimes.

List also reported that, in the late winter and spring of 1842, there had been a spate of theft and housebreaking in Dalkeith. On his advice, the Duke of Buccleuch and some of the inhabitants had raised a subscription to hire a brace of watchmen at fourteen shillings (70 Pence) a week, answerable to List. The watchmen had patrolled the streets, and over the year they had found and reported fifty-two doors, shutters or windows open, while many known thieves and prostitutes had been found "prowling about at an unseasonable hour." The latter were hauled in and held overnight. Since List had placed the watchmen on the streets, there had only been one housebreaking, and that was on a property outside their rounds. The County Constable seized the thieves later the same morning, and the watchmen recognised them as having been on the streets the previous night.

By 1849, when the county of Midlothian covered 350 square miles in extent (in 2020 it was 136 square miles,) there were still only 31 police officers to control crime. In the year between the First of July 1848 and the 30th June 1849, there had been 594 convictions, with 444 males and 150 females. That had fallen from 647 the previous year. There had been 241 convictions for theft, 91 for assault and breach of the peace, 71 for simple assault, one for stabbing, one culpable homicide, 26 for theft and housebreaking and 38 for poaching. All the time, List's war on beggars continued. As the Hungry Forties reached its climax and potato crops failed in Ireland and the Highlands, the County police ejected 1648 beggars, with 107 English, one from outside the United Kingdom, 625 Scots and 915 Irish. The police were doing their job, and List remained as Chief Constable of Midlothian until his retirement in 1877. He died at home in Edinburgh in 1883, aged 85.

List had put the Midlothian police on a secure footing with a force that was efficient for the county's crimes. That did not mean that life was trouble-free for the inhabitants.

Chapter 6

THE NAVVIES

On Thursday 7th May 1846, the landlord of the Arniston Inn stood nervously at the bar of Dalkeith Justice of the Peace Court. Accused of allowing his customers to descend into "disorderly conduct," he explained that it was hardly his fault that he had some of the rowdiest roughs in Scotland as customers. The Justices of the Peace listened to his protests, nodded and called on Sergeant Brown and Sergeant Little of the Railway Police to give their evidence. The police gave their opinion that the Arniston Inn was "the worst conducted house in the district" and mentioned they had frequently been called there to quieten the various disturbances that took place.

The sergeants consulted their notebooks and stated that around midnight on the 15th April that year they had been called to quell a disturbance in the Arniston Inn. When they arrived, they found a man slumped by the door and bleeding from the mouth; he said that a group of drunken railway labourers had attacked him. The police would sigh and look at each other, knowing that there was not much they could do except try and calm things down. They would give grim little nods when they heard that the Arniston Inn might lose its licence, but they knew that the troublemakers would only go elsewhere. By that time, the local police were pretty fed up with the railway labourers, or the railway navvies as they were popularly known.

The name "navvies" came from the eighteenth century when thousands of labourers dug and carved out the excellent canal network that was the cutting edge of transport technology of the time. Another name for the canals was the "inland navigations" so the men who dug them were known as "navigators," which soon became shortened to navvies. These navvies earned a fearsome reputation for their drunken rampages on pay-day and passed both their name and their character onto their successors, the labourers who created the world's first railway network by hacking out cuttings and raising bridges the length and breadth of the country. If anything, history remembers the railway navvies better than their predecessors, possibly because they are closer to us in time, perhaps because there were more of them or even because newspapers and court reports recorded their behaviour.

When the railways probed into Scotland, the railway navvies came with them. One of Scotland's earliest was the so-called "Innocent Railway" between Dalhousie Mains and St Leonard's in Edinburgh. The major shareholders for the railway were the same men who owned the coal mines: Sir John Hope, the Marquis of Lothian, John Grieve, the factor for the Duke of Buccleuch, and the family of Dundas of Arniston. Their line was built to carry coal from the Midlothian pits to the fuel-hungry fire-places of the capital. As these early lines were created before the days of steam-railways, horses hauled the carriages, but first, the line had to be dug. In common with all other railway lines, the work was hard and dangerous, with accidents among the workforce. For example, in April 1828 two Irishmen, Archibald McCorkindale and Daniel McBryde, died when an embankment on which they were working collapsed and fell in on them. McBryde was a widower with four dependent children, which heightens the poignancy of these hard-working men, losing their lives, working in Scotland. The navvies had a bad reputation, but they earned every penny the contractors paid them.

There were three or perhaps four distinct groups of navigators. The first was the Irish, who seemed to have the worst reputation, which may be undeserved. At that time, the press was noticeably down on the Irish who came across to Britain either as temporary workers or because famine and lack of opportunity drove them across the Irish Sea. There were religious and cultural differences as people from a predominately Roman Catholic and rural background tried to settle into a rapidly industrialising and urbanising, mainly Protestant, Britain, while many were desperately poor and spoke only Gaelic. It perhaps illustrates the dark side of human nature that they were looked on with some scorn and often fear before they assimilated into the mainstream of society. Irish navvies probably participated in most of the engineering work across the country.

The second group were the English navvies, often from the northern English counties and notorious for savage fighting, whether they were drunk or sober. They would make up the majority in Britain overall, but when the engineering works were in Scotland, they were less in numbers than the Scots or Irish. Then there were the Scots, whom we may divide into Highland and Lowland. The former more often worked in the northern half of the country, except when they came south for work and much the same reasons as the Irish. The famine of the 1840s affected the Highlands as well as Ireland, and there were thousands of hungry Highlanders hoping the man of the house could find work and wages working on the railway.

With such diverse and mutually antagonistic groups working on the same task, the contractors had no choice but to keep the various nationalities apart. Scots would work in one section of the line, Irish in another and the contractors would often place the English in between. When not working, the navvies would either be billeted in various lodging houses in the nearest settlement or would be in encampments of their own. Their huts were usually turf-roofed, with basic interiors that held rough beds and little else. These cabins could hold anything from a dozen men to half a dozen families where the navvy had his wife and children with them. When the line moved, these temporary encampments would travel with them, a creeping source of trouble and noise, accompanied by the obvious health hazards left behind by a hundred or more humans camped in places with, at best, rudimentary sanitary arrangements.

By 1846, Midlothian was well used to the unruly behaviour of navigators. Back in the summer of 1840, the Midlothian, or Edinburghshire Constabulary was in an embryonic state, and Superintendent Alfred List was renowned as being hard on vagrants and other people of no fixed abode. At that time, the railway line between Edinburgh and Glasgow was being created, and the navvies had the notion that List included them in the vagrant category. Accordingly, they retaliated first by organising a demonstration in Dalkeith. There was a minor riot with a couple of navvies arrested. As so often in the nineteenth century, an arrest led to an attempt to free the prisoner, and on that occasion, the police, helped by a posse of locals, lifted three more navigators.

To add insult to incarceration, List also banned the navigators from owning dogs while they were within Midlothian. That may sound harsh, but dog-fighting was popular among certain sections of the population, and often led to gambling and attracted members of the criminal fraternity to the area.

So when the Edinburgh to Hawick railway line came close to Gorebridge in Midlothian, the local population got ready for trouble. Parents would advise their sons not to emulate the navvies' drinking, swearing and smoking habits, mothers would sternly warn their daughters to stay well away from these frightening but possibly alluring invaders, and the police would take deep breaths and hope the navvies did not remain too long or do too much damage. Only the publicans may have rubbed their hands in glee at the thought of the extra revenue a few hundred thirsty navigators could generate ... As long as they behaved themselves.

In February 1846, the North British Railway was a major player in the United Kingdom railway network. Its lines extended across the country, and it employed thousands of men, both in engineering work and in running the trains that made such a massive difference to the lives of people. The 1840s were known as the Hungry Forties, after a succession of wet summers and bleak winters caused famine, so the navvies who worked on the Hawick line lived in miserable conditions which aggravated their natural truculence. In total there were over five thousand navigators in Midlothian at the beginning of 1846, some working on the Hawick line and others on the route to Glasgow.

As usual, with a multinational workforce, the contractors kept the different nationalities apart. The Scottish workforce under contractors named Graham and Sandison, and with a sprinkling of English to add salt, was based in the southern, Hawick section of the line, cutting and building the railway toward Edinburgh. Contractors named Wilson and Moore managed a smaller number of Irish on the northern section, pushing down toward the Borders. While a few Irish lodged in Dalkeith or Gorebridge, most lived in encampments around Crichton, with some huts holding twenty-four families who ate together and slept in bunk-beds that were slotted one on top of the other. There was no privacy and precious little comfort, while the food often came from "Tommy-shops" - shops run by the contractors that offered inferior quality products at high prices.

On the last Saturday of February, the Irish crowded into the then-small village of Gorebridge to be paid. When some men complained that the contractors cheated them of the wages they were due, the navvies were not in the best of fettle. Growling, they dissipated into the local change-houses and inns to spend their money in the manner they understood best. It would be a publican's dream, a captive clientele of thirsty labourers, all with wages burning a hole in their pockets.

A score of navvies piled into Somerville's pub in Gorebridge, relishing the warmth as well as the camaraderie. Some might have been singing, with high humour at the end of the working week, and then a packman followed them in. Packmen were peddlers, men who walked the highways and byways of old Scotland selling door-to-door and carrying news and gossip as well as small items that were not always locally available. In this case, he was peddling watches and may have thought that a bunch of newly-paid navvies would be so drunk they would buy anything. Instead, one of the navvies decided to keep the watches and not pay for them. Perhaps it was a misguided attempt at humour or a genuine theft, but either way, it began a sequence of events that ended in riot and murder.

Once it became evident that the grinning navvies had no intention of returning his watches, the packmen reported the crime to the local police office. Sergeant Brown of the Railway Police and Constable Christie of the County Police pushed into Somerville's, arrested two men they suspected of being the thieves and escorted them to the cells. Job done, they would breathe a sigh of relief at having escaped so lightly and settle down for what they hoped was an incident-free night.

The navvies, however, had other ideas. The press and police reports are at variance over precisely what happened next, but there is no doubt of the main facts. A considerable crowd of navigators, estimated at anything between 150 and 300, collected pick-axes, billhooks, spades and other weapons, and at about half past one in the morning, marched en-masse to the Gorebridge police office. Sergeant Brown and Constable Christie tried to outface them, and then to outmuscle them, but the navvies were determined, angry and in overwhelming strength. They barged into the office, felled Christie with the back of an axe and demanded that Brown release his prisoners. The sergeant refused, standing bravely in front of the roaring, gesticulating mob. Even when one of the navvies produced a pistol and thrust it at his head, Brown did not give in, although the navigator threatened, he would "blow your brains out." As a handful of navigators held Brown, others pushed past, smashed their pick-axes at the door of the cell, levered it open and withdrew in triumph with their released colleagues.

As the police licked their wounds, the navvies made merry through the streets of Gorebridge, with the no-doubt terrified inhabitants huddled behind shuttered windows and locked doors. The navvies let the locals know that they were victorious, parading their released colleagues and shouting and hooting as they marched. It was one of the nightmares of a small rural community to have a navigators' "randy" taking place in their village, but worse was to come for the people of Gorebridge.

Probably glad to be away from the vigilance of their sergeant, Constable John Veitch and thirty-year-old Constable Richard Pace were checking the country change-houses and pubs, walking from place to place to ensure there was no significant trouble. As they passed the hamlet of Fushie Bridge, (now Fushiebridge) they heard the swelling roar of a mob of navigators rampaging toward them. Deciding that, in this case, discretion was by far the better part of valour, the two men promptly hid behind a hedge. They would not know that this mob were the same men who had lately freed their comrades from the Police Office in Gorebridge and were now on their triumphant way back to their ramshackle huts hard by the Tyne Water at Crichton.

The navvies found the two officers and hauled them out of their hiding place, shouting "murder the police" and began to kick the constables to pieces. Pick handles swung, boots and fists flew, and the navvies knocked the police to the ground. Veitch managed to scramble to safety, but when somebody smashed a pick-axe handle on Pace's head, he lay there, stunned as the heavy, metal studded navvy boots went in. His wife, at home a bare hundred yards away, must have heard the commotion, but she would not know that the navvies were murdering her husband so close to home.

Leaving Pace a bloodied, dying mess, the navigators continued their noisy progress, now heading for the toll bar at Arniston. When it was safe, two local youths carried Pace home and left him with his wife before running to fetch the local doctor. There was little the doctor could do but make Pace as comfortable as he could. The constable lay still, as his wife watched and wept. With his skull fractured and his body covered in bruises, Pace, a man from the west coast, died that same day.

In the meantime, Superintendent Alfred List called up all the men he could: twenty-four uniformed police was an insufficient force, so he requested reinforcements from Edinburgh. Captain Haining of the City of Edinburgh Police sent down twenty-five officers who arrived in

Gorebridge to find the village tense with apprehension. The combined police force arrested thirteen of the Irish navvies in one day, and nine more the next, but the police only accused these men of rioting and not of the killing of Richard Pace. At that time, the police had no idea who had committed the murder. They offered a reward of £50 - a year's wages for a working man – for information leading to an arrest.

In the meantime, news had spread of the riot and murder. The Scottish navvies down in the Borders decided that they had to do something about these interlopers in their country. The previous year there had already been trouble between Scots and Irish in Fife, when the Scottish navigators pinned up notices warning "all the Irish men" to get "off the grownd and owt of the country... Or els we must by the strength of our armes and a good pick shaft put them off... Schots men." In the event, the threats in Fife came to nothing and the work continued with both nationalities involved. However, the memory and resentment remained, and now the Scots on the Hawick section of the line gathered to avenge this perceived slur on their national honour.

Around a thousand Scottish navigators, led by a bugler and a piper, left their work and marched northward toward the Irish at Crichton. An unknown number of English joined them, not caring about the provocation but always willing to join in a free fight. It was Monday, two days after the riot and murder and the Scots were out for blood. The tramp of their distinctive heavy "navy boots" would shake the surrounding countryside like the drumbeat of an invading army and the motley array of weapons they carried, pick shafts, hammers and cudgels, gave out an ominous warning of their intent.

Not surprisingly, news of their advance preceded the navvies, and the Midlothian police wondered how they could cope with this new force of aggressive railway labourers. Even when reinforced to double their number by the Edinburgh police, they would be hard-pressed, so the Midlothian force did what many police forces did throughout the century: they appealed to neighbouring police forces for help, and then to the army.

The Edinburgh police responded at once. They packed a coach-and-four with officers and sent it rattling south to Gorebridge. It must have been a dramatic scene with the blue-coated men jammed inside the swaying coach, holding onto their tall hats and truncheons as the driver cracked his whip and the horses cantered over the road. The men would know all about the riot and the death of one of their own; more used to the pub-brawls and petty thefts of Edinburgh's wynds and closes, they would wonder exactly they were facing in the wilds of Midlothian.

The army, however, had vast experience in dealing with civil disturbances. In the days before organised civilian police, the first line of defence was the military. It was not a role that made them popular as they put down riots in cities and supported the authorities against smugglers and political dissent. Now the 4th Irish Dragoons, the Blue Horse or the Mounted Micks at Piershill Barracks prepared to mount up and ride to prevent a dangerous confrontation between navvies of their own country and a growing mob of Scots.

And the Scottish army was growing. Around nine o'clock on Monday morning, the thousand-plus column of Scottish navvies halted at the paper mills at Newbattle, a couple of miles away from Gorebridge. They were organised and angry, and here around one hundred and fifty local colliers from the Marquis of Lothian's pits joined them, hard men, who had seen the Irish intruders run rampant around their area for too long. The combined force numbered an estimated 1,500 men: all tough, muscular grafters and all determined to exert revenge on the Irish.

The Scottish navvies headed straight for the Irish camps at Crichton Moss, no doubt hoping to beat up as many men as possible. They marched on, confident in their numbers, with the pipes screaming their battle-lust. The Irish were equally aware of their approach and mustered to meet them, three hundred fighting Irishmen who had already run riot in Gorebridge and murdered a policeman. And then they saw the numbers that opposed them.

Outnumbered around five to one, the Irish quickly lost their martial bravado, turned and ran. Perhaps some of the Scottish invaders followed them into the wild moorland around Crichton Castle, but the majority concentrated on the now-undefended encampment the Irish had left behind. The Scots did not touch the women or children that the fleeing Irish abandoned. Instead, they evicted them before they wrecked the Irish settlements and then put what remained to the torch. With Crichton Moss destroyed the Scots moved on to the other Irish encampments near Borthwick and treated them the same way.

According to contemporary reports, the few police did not show to great advantage while this happened. They seemed to have been ineffectual, nearly panicking so that when the local Sheriff Jamieson asked List what they were doing, he could only reply they were: "taking care of themselves." In reality, the Edinburghshire Police had not been created to put down massed mob violence but to control vagrants, petty theft and the occasional disturbance in the local pubs.

Not content with their spoilage and arson, the Scots then searched for the Irish overseers; they caught two, Darbie O'Brien and Thomas Carrol, who had remained in their homes at a farm steading near Crichton Moss. There was a confrontation, and the overseers received minor injuries. Perhaps the Scots blood was up, or they were frustrated because the Irish navvies had cheated them of a major brawl, but they continued to hunt for prey. Next on their list was Thomas Martin, a contractor who lived in the inn at Fushie Bridge. A bunch of navvies invaded the inn, brushed Barbara Wilson, the proprietor, aside and swung a cudgel at Martin's legs. He ran, with the navvies grabbing him and tearing his shirt as he escaped. They chased him across the fields to Catcune Mill, where he took refuge inside a cottage. Waiting outside, the navvies contemplated setting the place on fire with Martin inside, decided against fire-raising, and left, with the contractor still cowering within the cottage walls.

When the flames of the camps died down, and the navigator army dispersed in noisy triumph, Sheriff Graham Spiers and the Edinburghshire Constabulary moved back. Although Spiers wanted peace in his shire, he was not devoid of sympathy for the navvies. He had thought the contractors pushed the men too hard for safety and believed the railway companies should be in some way responsible for imposing order, as well as religion and morality, on the workforce. Perhaps more important, however, was the effect on the people of his county "that such an exhibition of social life may have."

However, fine ideas and moral disapproval could not solve the problem, and neither could the presence of a mere handful of police. All they did was survey the blackened wreckage of the Irish navvies' homes, nod sagely and wonder what to do.

When the carriage of Sheriff Spiers growled up, with his escort of sixty men of the 4th Irish Dragoons, the navvies were long gone. Spiers did what he could; he had the cavalry mount patrols around the Irish camps and used them to support the police as they searched the public houses on the route from Gorebridge and Hawick. On that first day, they arrested nineteen navvies, with others lifted in the following days.

The presence of the cavalry helped nullify the possibility of further rioting, but the embers of rancour remained. On the Wednesday following the murder, Scots and Irish navvies clashed at Pathhead and an Irishman stabbed a Scot. His injuries served as a warning that trouble could erupt at any time. There was a further reminder when the Irish realised that the massive Scots army had returned to the Borders, so they gathered together for a counter attack. Around two hundred angry Irishmen banded together to head south, only to have the Irish Dragoons, their own countrymen, range up before them, sixty strong with sabre, discipline and iron resolve. The navvies backed down; there were no more manifestations of major trouble.

Meanwhile, Sheriff Spiers and the police had been searching for the men who murdered Constable Pace. By careful questioning, they had obtained names and descriptions. The police were looking for Patrick Reilly and Peter Clark. Reilly was a "stout" (well-made and muscular rather than fat) man of around five feet seven in height, aged perhaps forty with black whiskers specked with grey, a moleskin waistcoat jacket, trousers and waistcoat, blue bonnet and "large navie boots." Clark was younger, between thirty-five and forty, taller by a couple of inches, with sandy hair and whiskers, grey trousers, a blue jacket and again "large navie boots."

Even if the names were genuine, and there is no guarantee they were, the suspects could change them at will. The descriptions could fit a thousand or more men who worked on railways up and down the country. The police never caught these two men; perhaps other navvies knew who they were, but if so, they never gave them up.

The Scottish navigators were less fortunate than the Irish. The police charged nine with mobbing and rioting, fire-raising and assault, plus malicious mischief for both the attack on the Irish huts and the assaults on the contractors. Of the nine, one was named Henry Brown, which could be a Scottish or English name, while the others had names that were as Highland as peat: Shaw, Morrison, McCracken, Grant, Mackay, McLean, McKillop and McQueen. The judges sent them all to jail with terms that varied from eight months for Shaw to two years for Brown. In June, months after the initial troubles, the police dragged a contingent of four Irish navvies to the High Court, from where they travelled free of charge to Australia for a seven-year term.

That was undoubtedly the worst navigator riot in Midlothian, but it was not the only trouble in which the navvies were involved.

To pick a few: in February 1847, the navigators William Mann and Donald McIntosh were found guilty of assault and breach of the peace in Dalkeith and fined 40 shillings. Then in June that same year, four Dalkeith-based Irish navigators, including three men from the same family, assaulted Mr and Mrs Samuel Baird. The sheriff told them it was pointless to issue a fine as their work colleagues would "raise the money by subscription" amongst themselves, so he jailed all four for sixty days.

Two years after the Gorebridge affair, the navvies were at it again. This time they were causing trouble at Stow, then in Midlothian, although now it is part of the Scottish Borders. It was in July 1848 that the police heard a whisper that the navigators were planning a randy

– their word for a drinking bout. Superintendent List had no intention of allowing another riot so sent a strong detachment of twenty men to forestall any trouble. They arrived in the very early afternoon, took up abode in the school-house and made their presence known even before the navvies hit the pubs.

The police had learned from previous experience not to wait for the navvies to control the situation. As soon as the noise levels in one of the pubs warned them that the trouble had started, the police entered in force. The navvies responded with a general attack, but in complete contrast to their behaviour at Crichton Moss, the police drew their truncheons and, as the press put it, "charged with such resolution and effect as to put their opponents to flight." The baton charge was sufficient to end the problems. The navvies dispersed without any more trouble and any need for a single arrest. In a way, dealing with the navigators had helped the Edinburghshire Constabulary come of age.

Chapter 7

RESURRECTION MEN

At five o'clock on the evening of 27th December 1822, one of the Marquis of Lothian's gamekeepers was returning to his home in the grounds of Newbattle Abbey. He was tired and frustrated, having spent the entire day hunting for poachers in his master's land, so when he heard movement in the kirkyard at Newbattle, he was tempted to ignore it. However, something persuaded him to investigate, and he saw three men working at a grave.

There were only two types of men who would do such a thing: gravediggers and grave robbers, the feared and hated resurrection men. It was too late for the former, and as the keeper watched, he realised that the men had dug into a new grave and were lifting the coffin that lay within. The keeper did not hesitate any further; in common with most people, he had a horror for grave robbers. Raising his flintlock musket, he thumbed back the hammer, took quick aim and fired.

The shot must have wakened the quiet village and certainly had its effect on the grave robbers. One of them shouted out "Murder! Murder!" and all three ran through the graveyard in a blind panic, with all thought of lifting the coffin forgotten. When the keeper inspected the site, he found a thin trail of blood marking their route and knew that he had hit one of them.

Such incidents were not uncommon in the eighteenth and early nineteenth centuries. At that time, Edinburgh was one of the leading medical centres of the world, with the medical school of the university rightly famous. Anatomy was an expanding science, with public lectures where students crowded round to witness human bodies being stripped of their dignity, skin and internal organs as the surgeon explained the use and position of each. Unfortunately, there were never enough legally obtainable bodies to meet the demand, so doctors turned a blind eye to other methods of supply.

The law stated that anatomists could only dissect executed criminals, orphans without an apprenticeship and un-christened babies. However, when the Government decided that many offences were no longer capital, the number of executions dipped and the supply of bodies faltered. Matters were different in other European countries, where anatomists could also legally dissect prostitutes after death. Anatomists needed bodies, and there were always unscrupulous men willing to find them – at a price. Body snatching was big business with a prime body fetching as much as £10. Now compare that to the average wage for a working man who would be lucky to pocket £1 a week and the temptations were obvious.

The body suppliers had various names, from the ubiquitous grave-robbers or body-snatchers to resurrection men and sack-'em-up men. Some criminals specialised in digging up the recently deceased to sell to anatomists, with others acting as "agents" who reported on new burials. Others were merely chancers, men who hoped to make a quick few shillings by digging up a recently buried corpse. Sometimes, they wished they had not.

In April 1742, Edinburgh was seething with anger. There had been cases of grave robbing in the area, which resulted in riots so that even the hardiest of resurrection men should have been reluctant to chance the Edinburgh mob. Even so, a man appeared at Potterrow Port, with a suspicious sack under his arm. When the city guard challenged him, the man dropped the bag and ran. Opening the sack, the guard found the body of a young boy, whom they soon discovered to be the lately deceased son of Robert Johnston, a periwig-maker. The boy had been buried at Pentland Kirkyard. The news rapidly spread, and somebody must have recognised the grave robber as John Samuel, a local gardener, for a mob soon rose and hurried to his house. Luckily for him, Samuel was not there, having fled, leaving his wife and children to face the fury of the crowd, who wrecked the house and stole everything they considered worth stealing, except Mrs Samuel's clothes and bedding. Although the mob was going to set the house alight, Mrs Samuel told them it did not belong to her husband, but a Captain Riddel and they drifted away, muttering what they would do to Samuel when they found him.

As the child's body was decently buried, this time in Greyfriars Kirkyard, John Coutts the Lord Provost of Edinburgh, issued a warrant and a reward for Samuel, with the city guard as well as the local population hunting for him. Eventually, the City Guard hauled Samuel before the court as his tearful wife watched and the people bayed for his blood. The judge ensured that the people had their wish, for he ordered the common hangman to whip Samuel through the streets of Edinburgh. After that, the judge banished Samuel from Scotland for seven years. Banishment was a common punishment in old Scotland, either from the area, town or the country.

However, one example was not sufficient to scare away those who sought to dig for easy money. By the early nineteenth century, grave robbing was so widespread that there was genuine public alarm. In 1821, the Reverend W. Fleming of West Calder reported:

> *Few burial grounds in Scotland, it is believed, have escaped the ravaging hands of resurrection men; and it is reported that with respect to a church-yard not far from Edinburgh, that, till within three years ago, when the inhabitants began to watch the graves, the persons interred did not remain in their graves above a night and that these depredations were successfully carried on for nine successive winters.*

Naturally, the resurrection men were amongst the least popular of criminals. Partly this was because people did not wish to see their loved ones vanish from their graves, to be exposed naked and sliced open for the education and entertainment of a crowd of gawking students. However, there were also more profound, more spiritual reasons. At the time, there was a belief that when the dead were resurrected in Heaven, God would re-create the body as it had been on Earth. There were genuine fears that if an anatomist dissected a body, it could not be resurrected in its entirety so that the grave robbers were not merely taking away a loved one's physical remains, but also damaging their life in the hereafter. No wonder resurrection men were both despised and hated.

If they were careful, the grave robbers were not at risk of significant punishment, even if the police did arrest them, for taking away a dead body was only a misdemeanour. Only if they took the grave clothes or any object that relatives had buried with the body, could they be convicted of theft, which could lead to transportation to Australia.

However, people were not inclined to merely sit back and hope that the resurrection men left them alone. There were ways to protect the dead. The simplest method was to ensure that retrieving the recently buried was difficult by compacting the soil above the grave and adding a few layers of branches, which, as anybody who has ever dug up a tree by its roots knows, are murderous to dig through. A more expensive method was to place a mort-stone on top. A mort-stone was a massive slab that would take two men a large amount of effort to lift when grave robbing depended on speed and secrecy. Relatives would remove the mort-stone after a few days when the body it protected had decomposed too far to be of interest to any anatomist. Of course, the resurrection men had a solution: dig at the top of the stone, smash open the end of the coffin and drag out the body.

Then there was the mortsafe, which was too expensive for ordinary people to afford. The mortsafe was an iron cage placed around the coffin as it was buried and dug up later. The gravediggers must have loved interring bodies only to re-open the graves a few weeks later to drag out a massive iron cage, ready for the next burial. The wealthy, of course, had family crypts, family graveyards within graveyards, complete with stone walls and sometimes heavy, lockable doors with the family name inscribed above.

Most common and most practical were the practices of having a mort house in which the dead could be stored behind locked doors until they were too decomposed to be useful, and of actually standing guard over the graveyards. These two methods were often combined, with a mort house combining its function with that of a watchtower, in which the guards could shelter during the hours of darkness.

There are a number of these watchtowers throughout Midlothian, and they were needed. Although it may have been relatively pleasant to stand a watch in summer, waiting in a graveyard through the bitter rain of a November or December night would try the endurance and possibly the nerves of the toughest. The men would gather around dusk, armed with a musket, pistol or whatever else they could find, fortify themselves against the cold by a dram or three of (possibly smuggled) whisky and wait for any unwanted intruders.

Midlothian has a plethora of anecdotal stories that tell of the struggles between watchers and robbers. The oldest tale comes from the Old Pentland kirkyard at Damhead, where the *Caledonian Mercury* mentioned grave-robbing as early as 1742. The watchhouse from Old Pentland dates from the eighteenth century, presumably as a result of that robbery. It is at the gates, with a chimney that suggests the watchers would huddle around the fire, with hopefully at least one man looking over the graves inside. One of the easiest watchtowers to find, and arguably the most impressive, is situated at the burial ground in Dalkeith. This two-story octagonal building was erected in 1827 shortly before the murders of Burke, Hare and MacDougall further heightened fear of body snatchers. Dalkeith had a Committee for the Protection of the New Burial Ground, who also used mortsafes made by James McGill, a Dalkeith blacksmith. That same year William Thomson, the last man ever hanged in Dalkeith, was buried here.

According to local legend the gravedigger, William King, was approached by a man calling himself Brownlee, who offered a large bribe if King buried Thomson in a shallow grave so Brownlee could dig him up more quickly. The following year the local bellman, Thomas Brown was accused of being in league with the resurrection men; there was not sufficient evidence to prove anything, so it is entirely possible that Burke and Hares' murders had created suspicion about every gravedigger.

Other watchtowers still survive, at Glencorse and Newton. The watchmen used the church bell tower at Lasswade; others, including Penicuik and Newbattle, have been demolished. It's a pity that people have destroyed so much built history, although a very good thing that the necessity for these old watchtowers has passed away.

There are anecdotal stories from many of the graveyards around Midlothian. Although very few seem to have primary documental evidence, some tales are worth repeating as they give a flavour of the period, although they may be apocryphal. One comes from Fala, where watchmen fired at suspected grave-robbers, only to hit the minister's goat. Others are in a similar vein, good stories but perhaps embellished by time and imagination.

However, there is no doubt that grave robbing took place in Midlothian and that men waited night after night in the graveyards, some probably eager to defend the dead, while others enjoyed the conviviality of cheerful company around a sparking fire and a bottle of something sensible. And then came the horrendous murders of Burke, Hare and MacDougall.

Rather than going to the trouble of digging up dead bodies, Burke, Hare and MacDougall murdered people around Edinburgh's Cowgate and Grassmarket, so providing Dr Knox, the anatomist, with extremely fresh bodies. The eventual discovery and arrest of Burke and Hare horrified the nation and led to the passing of the Anatomy Act in 1832.

That Act eased restrictions so that relatives could donate bodies to anatomists, who could also dissect any unclaimed bodies. The Home Secretary was now responsible for licensing Anatomists, and the law forbade them from dissecting bodies until somebody identified them. Anatomists also had to keep legal records and were liable to government inspections. What had been a scourge of the country faded away surprisingly quickly and passed into folklore and night-time stories. The dead could at last sleep in peace.

Chapter 8

THE PENTLAND STILLS

Whisky is the life of man
Always was since time began.

The above lines come from a nautical song that nineteenth-century seamen would roar out as they hauled on a rope or toiled at the windlass. It is a song for ordinary people who knew the bite of a good whisky and the warmth that a dram of the barley nectar could produce on a bitter day on the high seas or a damp, dreich day along the dockside of any of Scotland's ports. Scotland boasts a few songs that include whisky, which may say more about the subtle nature of the drink than the drinking nature of the people.

Back in the fourth century, a wise man named Aristotle remarked that even seawater could be drinkable once somebody distilled it. Perhaps a wandering Gael picked up on his words and added the knowledge that cereals were healthy and spirits good to drink, or maybe the Gaels had everything all worked out without any input from a classical scholar.

Legend claims that whisky came to Scotland when the Gaels began to emigrate from Ireland around the fifth or sixth century AD and that may well be true. The early history is undoubtedly obscure, when whisky, from *uisge beatha*, Gaelic for water of life, competed with mead, ale and wine for popularity in Scotland. Whatever the antecedents, whisky, made from local barley and pure, sweet burn water was cheap, refreshing and effective so that, by 1494, even King James IV tippled what was to become Scotland's national drink. However, by 1579, distilling must have been so widespread that the use of barley for whisky imperilled food production, for the Privy Council, Scotland's parliament, passed an act that allowed only "Earls, Lords, Barons and Gentleman, for their own use" the power to distil whisky.

Scots being what they are, the people completely ignored the Act, learned how to circumvent authority by locating their small-scale stills in out-of-the-way places and continued distilling. The government quietly laid aside their prohibition and wondered instead how to raise money from this water of life. The first Scottish tax on distilling came along in 1644. The purpose was to raise revenue to fund the Scottish Army that was allied to Cromwell against King Charles I in return for Cromwell accepting Presbyterianism in England. After the Scots had helped defeat Charles, two things happened: Cromwell did not adhere to the treaty and the tax remained in place. Such is the result of placing faith in the word of politicians.

At the end of the eighteenth and the beginning of the nineteenth centuries, whisky drinking was more than a habit; it was a way of life. Elizabeth Grant in her *Memoirs of a Highland Lady* writes of whisky drinking as "the bane of the country" and adds that from "early morning till late at night an eternal dram drinking was forever going." Everybody from the poorest beggar to the richest in the land drank whisky, even children. With such a demand, it is no wonder that the illicit distillers ensured there was also a supply.

Whisky distilling is now a multi-billion-pound boost to the Scottish economy, but at that period the government frowned on distilling for two reasons. Firstly, it utilised grain at a time when the country needed every ear of barley, wheat and oats to feed a frequently-grumbling population. Secondly, much of the distilling in Scotland was illicit and contributed not a single penny to the exchequer. In Scotland, "we're all

Jock Tamson's bairns" was and is a well-known saying. However, the stage had been set, with authority frowning on the mass distillation of whisky while the elite consumed quantities of spirits themselves.

After the 1707 Union of the Scottish and English parliaments formed the United Kingdom of Great Britain, customs officers appeared in Scotland to stop both coastal smuggling and illicit whisky distillation. The Union was unpopular in Scotland, with a turbulent beginning including an attempted French invasion in 1708 and Jacobite Risings in 1715 and 1719. By 1725, popular disgust with the Union was widespread, particularly when the government imposed a tax of 3d a bushel on malt. When people in Glasgow saw this tax as a breach of the Union and took to the streets in a riot, the Army was called out and shot twelve people. Despite the discontent, the tax remained, one of a series designed to raise revenue for the government's wars. At that period, highlanders enjoyed their whisky so much that an impressed visitor, Captain Edward Burt, one of General Wade's engineers, stated that some gentlemen drunk up to four quarts at a sitting.

In 1782, there were over 1000 illicit stills captured – and that was one year in a campaign that lasted decades. In 1793, the French Revolutionary War began and the licence duty increased by 300% to £9. By 1797 it had risen to £54. Larger legal stills could afford the price, while smaller legal stills either gave up or did not purchase a licence and distilled illegally. Three years later, the duty doubled again, and, in 1803, increased to £162. With legal distilling so expensive, illegal distilling thrived. A rising population, an increasing demand for whisky and, with the death of the kelp trade and slow demise of cattle droving, created a situation where illicit distilling flourished. It provided jobs and income, and perhaps the excitement of jinking the gauger and chancing the military added spice to the business. Illicit distilling was seasonal, occurring when the harvest had been gathered, and men faced periods of enforced idleness.

Not only did the tax remain, but it also increased. There is a saying that "Work is the curse of the drinking classes," but Excise duty was and is undoubtedly the curse of the whisky distillers. For a time in the early nineteenth century, there was a virtual war in the country as illicit distillers carried their whisky to their urban markets and the government sent Excisemen, the army and even the navy to prevent them. There were bloody encounters among the glens, sordid murders in the straths and the crack and roar of gunshot disturbing the peace of the north, and even the south of Scotland.

Although most people recognise whisky as a Highland creation, Lowlanders also distilled the golden nectar. Midlothian, with its bustling industrial villages, its proximity to the market of Edinburgh and its areas of wild land, was a perfect place for illicit distilling, and there are many tales and stories of the Pentland stills.

It is the nature of the beast that most of the story of distilling is hidden. Illicit whisky makers did not write memoirs, and only a few that the excisemen and army caught and prosecuted had their history recorded in the police, newspaper or court records. The illicit distillers of Midlothian seem to be among the most successful as they appear in very few court cases. However, sometimes the newspapers carried stories of the forces of authority unearthing illicit stills. There was one such instance when the *Caledonian Mercury* of 27th October 1808 stated that an "illicit still was discovered at Lawrie's Den on Soutra Hill." In this case, the unnamed owner of the still created his own problems.

It seems that the distiller was a licensed carter as well as one of a group of men who had operated a still on the lower slopes of Soutra Hill. He had periodically taken his cart into Dalkeith to buy casks to hold his whisky, but in September of that year, he had taken away a cask without bothering to pay. The cooper noticed, and the next time the distiller returned, demanded his money.

The distiller pleaded his total innocence of the theft and added insult to criminality by refusing to say who he was or from where he came. That was enough for the good people of Dalkeith: The distiller was arrested and locked securely in the tolbooth while investigations continued. They checked his cart, where the license gave his address as Lawrie's Den.

The address rang some alarm bells: Why would anybody from such an isolated spot regularly buy empty casks? The only possible reason was to fill them with something, and the man's refusal to give his name added fuel to the speculation that he was an illicit distiller. An excise officer rode to Lawrie's Den to scour for the still. He found evidence including a few casks of wort, which was the liquid drained from the mash tun, the receptacle in which the distiller mashed malted, and he found un-malted barley with water.

Lawrie's Den was a perfect place for a still. The name came from a public house that once stood there, owned by a man named Lawrie. It was a wild place, where carters, drovers and other wanderers gathered to drink and fight. It was also allegedly the scene of a murder when two groups of gypsies fell out. To the north was a small hut that was the home of a reputed witch named Margaret Dobson. Strangely, that seemed to be the end of the matter. Either there was not enough evidence or the crime was hidden behind another. However, the case was symptomatic of a network of such illegal operations that today only folklore remembers.

A short step from the southern frontier of Midlothian and just inside the Borders is Carlops, allegedly named after the Carlin's Loup – the witches jump. Nearby there is a place known as the Steel. It is a lonely house situated in a loop of the Harlawmuir Burn and looks on to the Harlaw Muir and beyond to Auchencorth Moss. In the nineteenth century, there was little sound here but the sough of the wind, the hiss of heather and the bubbling call of the whaup. The Steel was also the home of John and Mary Cairns.

At that time Carlops was a weaving community, each little cottage in the single main street tenanted and busy with looms clacking from the back room. Handloom weavers were prosperous, and there was the excitement of a daily coach rattling through to Edinburgh and the biannual fun of a fair. John Cairns realised that a little private enterprise was in order and, teaming up with a weaver from nearby Monkshaugh, he began to distil his own whisky.

An illicit still is easy to hide in the fold of a moor, where drifting mist can mask the smoke, but the distinctive aroma is less easy to disguise. When it became evident that Cairns was making money and the government was not, the gaugers – excise men – came a-calling. There were no secrets in rural villages, and some helpful person informed Cairns that he was about to be raided. Assisted by the Monkshaugh weaver, Cairns grabbed all his equipment, dragged it to the moor and buried it. In the meantime, the gaugers had arrived at his house.

Smack in the open and hard by the door, a barrel of newly made whisky stood brazen and defiant with its bung-hole open for all to inspect. The gaugers were in the house, rummaging for evidence of law-breaking, but Mary Cairns was a woman of wit and resource. She had been pouring soor-dock – buttermilk – through a filler, and now she disguised the whisky barrel by placing the filler, smeared as it was with milk, into the open bung-hole. For some reason, the gaugers did not smell the whisky, ignored the now seemingly innocuous barrel and left the house, suspicious but empty-handed.

John Cairns was pleased to be at liberty but less happy when Mary insisted that one such escape was enough. With at least one unpleasant neighbour willing to report them, and the gaugers now suspicious, distilling would be harder in future. John took the advice of his astute wife and abandoned his attempt at Free Enterprise. There was no more distilling at the Steel.

Further north, at Swanston, there was a distiller at Bowbridge. According to Robert Louis Stevenson, who knew the area very well and may have got the story from John Tod, the local shepherd, there was also a solitary gauger. This government official was a cheery man who played the flute as he rode up to Bowbridge, with the Craigs of Caerketton lowering overhead and sweet Allermuir thrusting behind. He played "Over the hills and far away," which distinctive tune alerted the distiller to his presence. In common with so many people, the distiller was not averse to bending the law now and then if it got in his way. Accordingly, when he heard the gauger's flute, he loaded the bulk of his stock onto a cart and trundled it to the back of Caerketton.

The distiller must have been a fast driver, or the gauger was very slow, for when the gauger arrived at his house, the distiller was ready to meet him. The gauger checked all the visible barrels of whisky and charged the required duty. After that, it was a companionable dram by the fire with neither man mentioning the uncounted and untaxed barrels hidden in the hills. One wonders if the gauger played his flute as a warning.

Around 1820, there was a small still at Marfield, a farm in the Walstone Muir on the fringes of the Pentlands. With a companion from Ninemileburn, the farmer ran his still and sold the excess to the good neighbours of Penicuik and possibly to the burghers of Edinburgh, ten miles or so to the north. The Marfield distillery earned a particular reputation for the quality of its product, and the gaugers became regular visitors as they searched for the still.

These old-time stills consisted of the still itself, which was generally of copper and stood on a furnace of loose stones. A coil, known as a worm, condensed the liquid and dripped it into a receiver that could be something as homely as a locally made earthen jar with a simple lid. There was also a mash-tun and, of course, a source of running water. In Scotland, there was never any shortage of running water. The illegal stills were often underground, with a pipe leading from the furnace to the surface, or the distiller placed them inside a rough bothy of dry-stane walls, roofed with heather or turf that helped dissipate both the smoke and the aroma. The gaugers searched the moors for wisps of smoke and hoped to smell the throat-catching sweetness of whisky, but the Midlothian moors often holds mist in pockets and folds of land and the perfume of whisky has rivals in heather scent carried by the whispering wind. It was no easy task for the revenue men, and they never did find the still at Marfield.

Quite aware of their success and mindful of the fact that without solid proof there could be no convictions, the Marfield farmer one day approached the gaugers and remarked that it was a shame that so much searching had achieved nothing. When the gaugers agreed, the farmer invited them into his house for something to eat. As it was a blustery day and the excisemen were soaked and chilled from ploutering through the sodden moor, they agreed, and the guidwife fed them well. She also dispensed homemade spirits to warm them up, and the gaugers drank happily, seemingly bearing no resentment that the whisky had paid no duty.

Then there was Robert Scott. He was a Carlops man with no wife to keep him on the path of righteousness or help him at the still. He was well known in the illegal distilling world yet was surprised when a body of gaugers travelled down from Edinburgh and came straight to his headquarters. Presumably, they had been given advance information, for the gaugers, like the police, operated through a network of informers. They raided Scott's still at Stonypath, where the Roman Road ran parallel to Windy Gowl, and the River Lyne provides clear Pentland water for the whisky.

The gaugers showed no mercy to the apparatus. They destroyed jars and tuns, then loaded the worm and copper still onto a cart, to carry it to Edinburgh. Perhaps Scott was watching, fuming with frustration as the government men trundled onto the old rutted road and moved slowly northward past Linton Muir and Carlops, Honeybrae and Spittal until at Ninemileburn they stopped for a quick snack and something to clear the dust from their throats.

Thomas MacLean was the landlord of the inn at Ninemileburn, and in the past, he had accepted much of Robert Scott's duty-free whisky. He listened to the boasting of the excisemen, saw the equipment tied to the cart and said, loudly:

"If ony lass wants a new ribbon, now is her chance if she cuts that string."

As anybody who has read Jane Austen knows, young girls at the beginning of the nineteenth century loved ribbons as fashion accessories, and Helen Barr, one of the serving girls, decided that a new ribbon would be very acceptable, thank you kindly, Mr MacLean. She followed the cart as it left Ninemileburn, waited until it slowed for a rise in the road, dashed forward, sliced the hempen cord that held the distilling equipment secure and scampered away before the gaugers caught her.

One by one, the precious articles fell to the ground, and in the dim of the evening, the locals liberated them. Soon Rob Scott had his still back in working condition, and there was cheap whisky for the Inn at Ninemileburn.

One still that was locally famous and seemed set to challenge even Glenlivet for the quality of its produce was at Garvaldsyke in the Pentland Hills. Garvaldsyke was on the southernmost border of Midlothian, where Tweeddale and Clydesdale merged, which gave the still an enviable advantage over others. With Peebles, Lanark and Edinburgh all within a seventeen-mile radius, the distillers of Garvaldsyke had three ready customer bases for their whisky. They also had an excellent supply of water as the source of the South Medwin Water ran sweetly past.

Whoever selected this spot for a still knew what he or she was doing. At that time, the opening decades of the nineteenth century, the government had not accurately determined the boundaries of the three counties, so any local authorities had to be careful they did not step onto a neighbour's territory. Garvaldsyke is also an excellent place for security, with bogland all around making it all-but inaccessible for anybody who did not know the secret paths and dry spots. While most stills had some form of shelter, the still at Garvaldsyke was entirely in the open, with the distillers relying on their remote location to protect them from the excisemen. There was the additional security of being able to see people coming a long way off. Three men worked the still here, and the business boomed.

The still was said to use up to eighteen bolls of malt every week, with the whisky selling at eighteen shillings a gallon. One elderly man was continually at the still, with two younger men taking the whisky on horseback to sell in the towns, and buying coals for the still as well as the malt, at £2 five shillings a boll. Every night one of the distillers slept by the still, using a vat for shelter, with its bottom facing the wind. When the winter snow came, the watcher slept, or lay, with his feet closest to the furnace.

When the horses were not busy carrying whisky, they sheltered at the nearby Little Vantage Inn. For a while, the local farmers walked wary of the smugglers, but once they realised how high quality the whisky was, they refused to touch the stuff from Glenlivet and other Highland places, and demanded only "the true Garvaldsyke." Even the highlanders, down for the autumn harvest, seemed to prefer the Pentland distillation rather than the whisky from the north. If that situation had continued, it is possible that the future Scottish whisky industry could have centred itself in Midlothian rather than Speyside and Moray.

In early 1814, the excisemen finally learned where the still was and decided that nothing less than a full raid would work. Whistling up a section of soldiers, the excisemen marched through the Pentland Hills and arrived at the bogland around the still. Either they had a local informer, or the exciseman was skilled in hill-craft for he led his redcoats straight through the moss to the site of the still. However, the distillers had their own intelligence network and must have learned that the gaugers were after them. They had cleared the site and left, so the excisemen found only a couple of battered old vats.

One final Pentland tale comes from Penicuik. Around 1810, some women stopped for a drink from the water spout at the Delve Brae. This water had an exquisite taste, and the workers lingered, sampling more and more until they realised that they were no longer completely sober. Their boss at the paper mills noticed that his workers were a bit under the weather and made enquiries, lifting a curious eyebrow at the news of this unique well. Naturally, the news spread, and before the day was out, there was an exodus to examine the mysterious phenomenon of a whisky spout. The water in the spout was found to contain spirits, and a thorough search unearthed an illicit still with a leaking barrel of whisky. The still was destroyed but, as so often, the gaugers did not seem have traced the owners.

Of course, not all the illicit spirits were from whisky stills. In the eighteenth century, Scotland was also notorious for smuggling in spirits and goods from abroad. The Union of 1707 did not just merge Scotland's parliament with that of England and Wales; it also introduced new customs and excise laws into Scotland. Until that time, such things were barely known and certainly not enforced. After 1707, a whole new breed of customs and excise officials swarmed over the country, creating all sorts of difficulties for seamen trying to make a now-dishonest living. Scottish fishermen were as apt to spend their times carrying duty-free goods, with the now-gone fishing community on the Isle of May notorious for smuggling.

As Midlothian did not have a coastline, there was no direct smuggling from the county, which did not mean the people were not affected. In April 1735, the excisemen, aided by a party of the military, seized two cart-loads of brandy plus seven pack-horses laden with French spirits just outside Dalkeith. The *Caledonian Mercury* commented that "the incredible Number of Seizures lately made… must convince the World of the pernicious effects of Smuggling." The World may have been convinced, but to the ordinary people of Scotland, struggling under the lash of poverty, excise duties meant higher prices than they could afford. Smugglers were not unpopular in old Midlothian.

Throughout the period of whisky wars, the government tried every method to close down the illicit stills and smugglers. From high fees on every still to allowing only large stills, to a considerable duty on whisky and using the Army as a blunt instrument to bludgeon the whisky makers into submission, they gradually realised that they might win in one area, but the native wit of the Scots always found another. In 1822, with the army still roaming the country, the government asked for a £10 licence fee and slashed the duty. Smuggling and illicit distilling did not die out overnight; indeed, there is still peat-reek today, but the authorities had broken the back of the problem. New, legal distilleries sprung up, and Scotland gained an industry that spread her fame around the World. The whisky war gradually ended, and the government withdrew the military from that long drawn out intermittent campaign. The stories remain, but people have forgotten the sheer scale of operations against illicit distilling.

Today Scotland is famous for its whisky, with distilleries from Pencaitland in East Lothian to Orkney. Undoubtedly there will be some illegal distilling somewhere, maybe even in Midlothian for in the words of perhaps the most famous Exciseman of all time: "freedom and whisky gang together."

Chapter 9

THE MILITARY IN MIDLOTHIAN

Soldiers appear throughout this book, peering out of the pages in small vignettes, either as men breaking the law or as men helping the police maintain order in the community or aiding the gaugers hunt for whisky smugglers. In Midlothian, the main military base was just outside Penicuik, but it may be best to look at the historical British soldier before moving to Penicuik itself.

In the eighteenth century, Britain fought one major war after another, with France as the main adversary, but Spain, the Netherlands and the United States offering alternative enemies, depending on the whim of politics and alliances. In the nineteenth century, most wars were on the fringes of the Empire, but in all cases, the man at the sharp end of government policy wore battered scarlet and served for a pittance. The newspapers and history books lauded his courage and determination, but respectable people would still cross the road to avoid the British soldier.

However profuse the praise, the soldier's life was hard, often sordid and could vary from mind-numbingly tedious to terrifyingly perilous. He had more chance of dying of disease rather than in battle and was often treated with contempt by the very people he was in uniform to protect. Once a recruit accepted the King's or Queen's silver shilling, he stepped out of one world and into another. If he were fortunate, he would find a new family with close comrades and a career. If he were unfortunate, he could be the victim of harassment by sergeants, vicious bullying and savage punishments. He would probably learn to drink heavily and brawl with civilians or other regiments; he would embrace regimental pride and be trained to move at the word of command. The Empire was his oyster, and he could be posted anywhere from the deep snow of Canada to the stifling heat of Burma, from the unbelievable beauty of Southern Africa to the fever islands of the West Indies. He might be incredibly fortunate and never face an enemy, or he could have a hard career and face French or Russian artillery, Burmese dacoits, Pashtun jezzails and Africa assegais. The soldiers expected hunger, knew they were virtually guaranteed hardship and accepted the various diseases of India as hazards of the job.

Above the soldier, issuing commands and in theory, looking after him, was a bevy of officers, men who lived in a different world.

Army officers could be from an aristocratic background, but most were the sons of country gentlemen. A few came through the ranks, men whose ability or bravery raised them above the usual social ceiling. Very few of these obtained field rank and only a handful reached the top of their profession. Through the eighteenth and for the first decades of the nineteenth century, most officers acquired promotion through purchase, that is by buying the rank of an officer who had died, been promoted or resigned his commission. Some newspapers even openly advertised commissions, such as this example from the *Caledonian Mercury* of 20th February 1800:

> *The Following Ensigncies at the Prices and on the Stations undermentioned are to be disposed of.* Apply to Mr Mason, no 1 Somers Place, London.
> In 3rd Regiment of Foot, St Kitts, West Indies £315
> 26th do, returning to England from America £350
> 27th do, England £350
> 43rd Do, on passage from West Indies to England £350

> 53rd Do St Vincent West Indies £315
> 63rd Do England £350
> 71st Do Scotland £350
> 75th Do East Indies £367 10/-
> No gentleman will apply with a view of obtaining them beneath the prices set down, or unless the gentleman for whom the commission may be wanted is sixteen years of age (the age limited by His Majesty's Regulation) and can procure a respectable recommendation.

Despite the efforts of the Duke of York, the system of purchase continued until the 1870s. Ridiculed in the children's nursery rhyme, the Grand old Duke of York, otherwise, Prince Frederick, Duke of York and Albany (1763 – 1827) was a career soldier who led the British Army in Flanders in two campaigns in the 1790s, with mixed fortunes. The Duke of York was more successful in reforming the administration when he became Commander-in-Chief. He founded the staff college and a "corps of Waggoners" that grew into the Royal Army Service Corps. He also founded the adjutant general's and military secretary's departments and laid the groundwork for a series of reforms that continued throughout the century, creating an army that very slowly became more efficient.

Not all soldiers were regulars. There was a bewildering array of part-time and semi-professional military units to defend the country and act as feeders for the units that faced whoever the enemy happened to be. That was particularly true during the French wars. There was the Militia, who were picked by ballot, although the rich could often persuade a less wealthy man to take their place, and augmenting the militia were the Fencibles. These formations dated back to 1759 during the Seven Years War and were revived in higher numbers from 1793 onward. The Fencibles were regulars but were raised only to defend Britain, although some helped garrison Gibraltar and many Scottish Fencible regiments served in Ireland during the 1798 Rising. There was also the Yeomanry, who were mounted and usually from rural areas, and the Volunteers that included infantry, cavalry and artillery. Some men soon found that they were not suited to military life, with this advertisement from the *Caledonian Mercury* only one of many:

> 05 March 1795
> Deserted
> From the Midlothian Fencible cavalry, lying at Kelso commanded by the earl of Ancrum, on the 14th February
> WILLIAM NASMYTH, Coal-hewer, born in the parish of Ormiston, and county of Midlothian, 30 years of age, five feet four inches high, pale complexion, brown hair, grey eyes, and well made. He is supposed to be lurking about in the neighbourhood of East-houses (where his wife and family reside) near Dalkeith.
> Whoever will secure the said William Nasmyth in to any of His Majesty's jails, shall receive a reward of Two Guineas, by applying to the Commanding Officer at Kelso, or to Mr Thomas Foggan at Dalkeith.

As the nineteenth century progressed and the Empire expanded, the soldier's lot grew ever more varied, and the conditions under which he laboured gradually improved. But soldiers were no angels. There were occasions when they rioted in the streets, or resorted to their recurrent vice of drink and became a public nuisance. The army could make itself extremely unpopular in Scotland, or it could be the focus of intense patriotism as regiments marched to, or returned from, various wars. That was the contradiction of Scotland's relationship to the soldiers in its midst. In Midlothian, there was a further complication as prisoners of war were brought here; the enemy existed in the middle of the people.

Annals of Greenlaw

When people drive past the spanking-new barracks of Glencorse, just outside Penicuik, or peer out of the window of a bus to see what the army are up to today, very few will realise that they are looking at a place whose military history stretches back for over two hundred years.

In the early eighteenth century, European wars achieved a veneer of civilisation. They were fought mainly by highly trained professional armies that depended on manoeuvres and tactics, and rarely involved civilians unless they were unfortunate enough to be on the route of marching armies. However, when battles did take place, they were as ugly and terrible as they always have been and, to the soldiers at the sharp end, the wars were bloody enough and army life brutal in the extreme. One thing that had improved was the treatment of prisoners of war. Rather than being sent into slavery or killed out of hand, prisoners were treated with some humanity and kept in prisoner-of-war camps. The system was not perfect but was an improvement on what had gone before.

During the French Revolutionary and Napoleonic Wars of the late eighteenth and early nineteenth century, Britain was fighting France and its allies. For most of that period, the majority of the enemy prisoners would be seamen captured by the Royal Navy, but when the British Army returned to the shores of Europe in the peninsular campaign, an increasing number of French and allied soldiers were captured and held as prisoners in the United Kingdom. Of the more than 120,000 prisoners in the decade before 1814, around 10%, 12,000 or so, were held captive in Scotland. These unfortunate men were imprisoned in Perth, Edinburgh Castle and three separate sites in Penicuik: Valleyfield, Esk Mills and Greenlaw House, that later became Glencorse Barracks.

For most of the war years, the prisons were reasonably quiet, but after 1811, the prisoner population exploded. That year there were rumours that French prisoners in the south of England planned to escape and seize control of the naval base at Portsmouth, to coincide with an invasion by Bonaparte across the Channel. This ludicrous conspiracy theory was enough to see the prisoner total of Penicuik rocket as the government distributed their captives throughout Great Britain.

Of the three sites that held prisoners of war, Greenlaw, was arguably the most historic. It was nearly two miles outside Penicuik, with the mansion of Greenlaw House converted to contain prisoners in the early years of the nineteenth century. In 1813, the army added additional buildings as the number of prisoners increased. The depot was completed shortly before the end of the war, when the government returned prisoners to their homelands. William Chambers described the camp as "a group of barracks, surrounded by tall palisades, for the accommodation of some hundreds of prisoners who, day and night, were strictly watched by armed sentries." Chambers visited on a Sunday and saw them "dressed in coarse woollen clothing of a yellow colour and most of them wearing red or blue cloth caps or partly-coloured cowls; the prisoners were engaged in a variety of amusements." One corner of the camp had a booth with "café de Paris" above the door, while others sold small prison-made articles through windows in the palisade.

While visitors to Edinburgh Castle can view the dungeons where French prisoners survived the war, Penicuik does not capitalise on that part of her history. Many people have heard of the 1811 escape from Edinburgh Castle, where scores of daring Frenchmen climbed down the Castle Rock with a rope and scattered around the countryside in their attempt to reach France. One man died, the authorities recaptured the others, but the memory remains. Very few people have heard of the dramas that took place in Greenlaw.

In the early years, most of the prisoners held in Greenlaw were seamen, and not all were as keen to sing *the Marseilles* as the men who escaped from Edinburgh. In July 1804, only a year after the prison depot opened, thirty-two of the prisoners decided that they preferred to serve with the Royal Navy, rather than languish in Greenlaw. All volunteered on board HMS *Roebuck*, which was a decision many might have regretted if the words of Dr Johnson are correct. He compared life at sea with that of being in prison, except with the added danger of drowning. However, these men were Prussians, Dutch and Flemings so were involved in a war where their nations played a fluid part at best. *Roebuck* had been launched as a 44-gun frigate, in 1774, but later became a guardship. It is possible that the prisoners-of-war were merely held there before being transferred to other vessels.

Sometimes, there were flashes of genuine humanity that remind us that the majority of people are decent even during wartime. With shipwrecks as frequent then as car crashes now, seamen were occasionally rescued by their wartime enemies. Early in 1807, a Dutch vessel came ashore on Orkney, and the survivors were taken prisoner and eventually ended up at Greenlaw. However, the government decided the Dutchmen were "seamen in distress" rather than prisoners of war and ordered them released. In April, the shipwrecked survivors were taken as passengers on board *Norfolk*, an armed ship (merchantman commandeered by the Royal Navy) where Captain Richan transported them to the Texel and set them free.

Things were not always so happy in the prisoner-of-war camp. Despite holding the lowest commissioned rank, Ensign Maxwell was in command of the thirty-six men of the Lanarkshire Militia who guarded the prisoners. On the 7th January 1807, Maxwell ordered the French prisoners to douse their lights. When the French did not respond, Maxwell ordered one of the sentries to fire into the room. There was the sharp crack of a musket, a jet of white smoke, the spurt of flame and the acrid stench of burnt gunpowder. The shot killed Charles Cortier, a Dunkirk seaman. The authorities took action, partly because they were not pleased with Maxwell's response and possibly also because the French might retaliate against the British prisoners-of-war they held. A sheriff officer arrested Maxwell, and his case came before the High Court in Edinburgh in June that year.

At his trial, Maxwell defended himself vigorously. He claimed that if his orders had caused death, then he had been justified in giving the order. He said that it had been his duty as an officer to keep the prisoners in control. The trial was long and complicated, lasting a full eight hours, followed by two more hours when the jury deliberated: was it a duty-officer's right to keep prisoners-of-war under control by force, or was it murder to order a sentry to fire into a room of unarmed men?

Eventually, the jury came to a decision. Maxwell had not acted in a premeditated manner, so it was not murder, but he had been responsible for Cortier's death. Maxwell was guilty of culpable homicide and sentenced to nine months in Edinburgh's Tolbooth.

There was a similar case later, when the prisoners became unruly and threw stones and rubbish at their sentries. Private James Inglis reacted badly, aiming his musket and firing through the window. His shot killed a Danish seaman named Simon Simonson. As with Ensign Maxwell, Inglis was arrested and appeared in court, where the jury found him guilty of culpable homicide. However, while the judge had sentenced Maxwell to a relatively light nine months in Edinburgh, Private Inglis had to endure fourteen years transportation to Australia for the same crime but with more provocation. It seemed there was one law for officers and another for men.

Not all the trouble concerned the prisoners. British soldiers were quite capable of bickering amongst themselves without enemy prisoners to provide an excuse. The British Army was proud of its regimental traditions, with every soldier owing loyalty to the Crown but individual regiments boasting their own history and treating their men like an extended family. Regimental rivalries were often long-standing, having arisen from some grievance decades before, and different units frequently dispelled frustrations in savage fights with fist, boot and belt buckle. Militia regiments were created to relieve the regular units of the onerous garrison and home defence duties and did not have the long list of battle honours of their regular brethren, but they did seem to adopt some of the traditions of prickly regimental pride. It was mainly Militia regiments who kept guard over the prisoners at Greenlaw, and on some occasions, their regional pride got in the way of military discipline.

On the 20th November 1806, the commanding officer of the Stirlingshire Militia sent Corporal William Dreghorn and another corporal from Penicuik to Greenlaw House with a personal message. On his short journey, they met some privates of the Lanarkshire Militia. After the initial pleasantries and insults, the two units proved regimental pride by coming to blows, with Dreghorn getting the worst of things. However, there was no significant damage done, and they parted with only dark mutterings and threats of future violence. Dreghorn reported the incident to his commanding officer, who brushed it off as unimportant and sent him back to Greenlaw House with another message. Possibly in an attempt to avoid any further trouble, the commanding officer ordered a sergeant of the Lanarkshire Militia to accompany him.

Either resentful of what happened on his previous encounter with the lads from Lanarkshire, or just ultra-cautious, Corporal Dreghorn brought his musket with him, ready loaded with ball cartridge. Although the sergeant strongly advised him against carrying a loaded musket, Dreghorn shouldered his piece and marched down the road in utter defiance, or perhaps he was bloody-mindedly looking for trouble.

If he was looking for trouble, he found it. At the small village of Kirkhill, Dreghorn and the sergeant ran into four men of the Lanarkshire Militia. As before, they exchanged words and regimental insults, and this time rather than a flurry of punches, Dreghorn levelled and fired his musket. The ball tore into Private William McLeay, hitting him low on the left side of his abdomen. McLeay fell at once, and the others stopped, shocked at the turn of events: Words and fists were one thing, muskets and ball ammunition quite another. McLeay died the next morning, and Dreghorn was arrested and charged with murder or culpable homicide.

He appeared before the High Court in February 1807. The trial lasted a full day before the jury decided that Dreghorn was not guilty. He was perhaps a lucky man, or maybe the court understood the passion forged by regimental pride.

The French prisoners were active and ingenious in their attempts to escape. In July 1813, a group of French prisoners managed to fix a false bottom onto one of the carts that carried the human waste from the camp. Three men squeezed in, and the cart drove out of the camp for some distance. When the driver stopped to talk to a friend, the three prisoners escaped and ran toward a nearby wood. An off-duty and unarmed soldier recognised what they were and grabbed the nearest escapee, who drew a knife and plunged it into the soldier's neck and side, gravely wounding him, and then ran on. However, the soldiers shouted an alarm and wrestled all three prisoners to the ground.

About five in the morning of the Tuesday before the 6th March 1811, 23 of the French prisoners at Eskmills escaped. They lifted the floorboards of their room and dug their way out of the camp. Unfortunately for them, three sentries patrolled between the camp and the River Esk and could hardly fail to see over a score of Frenchmen pop out of the ground. All three guards shouted a challenge, lifted their muskets and pressed the triggers. One soldier's musket misfired, the second missed, and the third hit his mark. The guards captured another five of the prisoners, but seventeen managed to escape into the Midlothian countryside, causing a manhunt that lasted for days.

The French prisoners of war were also an artistic body of men who created original works of art to sell to raise money. Unfortunately, they also used their talents to produce forged bank notes of a quality sufficiently high to fool even suspicious Scottish merchants. The French circulated these notes by giving them as change for products they made, or by buying items from the guards. In December 1813, Private Thomas Gray was with the Kirkcudbright militia at Penicuik when Major Gore ordered a search of the barracks for forged notes. Captain Dunn supervised the search, and as well as the forged notes he had found a letter that proved Gray had bought or sold articles of plaited straw from the prisoners. That was against regulations, so Dunn rummaged through Gray's possessions and found a selection of forged banknotes including two forged £2 notes of the Bank of England, and two forged £2 Bank of Scotland notes. Gray claimed he had found the notes near the stockade, the name given to the palings that surround the prison. He said he told nobody, not even his wife and did not try and spend them. His trial was on the 30th May 1814, and he pleaded not guilty. There was some doubt as to whether the law for forgery extended to Bank of Scotland notes, but the court decided that it did, unfortunately for Gray. Gray had been ten years in the regiment and had never been in trouble, but the court gave him the maximum fourteen years transportation.

Other Frenchmen made their mark in much more pleasant ways, as J. Black in *Penicuik and Neighbourhood* hinted that some of the French prisoners had become very friendly with the local women, with the inevitable result of half-French babies enhancing the local gene pool. There may have been some lingering remnant of the Auld Alliance as, more than once, local people fraternised with French prisoners-of-war. There was one case when Janet Hislop Delane and James Hislop aided three prisoners to escape. The prisoners, Frenchman Captain Pierre Martys, the German Charles Etain of the 17th Dragoons and the Frenchman Lieutenant Charles Foucald of the 26th Foot had been on parole in Lanark in 1813. Hislop and De Lane were arrested and tried at the High Court, which sentenced them to seven years for their pains.

The Battle of Waterloo put a bloody full stop to the French wars, and the prisoners-of-war were sent home as an unfamiliar peace descended on Europe. Once the Napoleonic war was over, the army rapidly shrunk as regiments disbanded. With no European war in which to collect customers, the Army had to find another use for its beautiful new buildings. In 1844 the government decided to have structured military prisons for offenders. In England, these were at Southsea Castle and Chatham, while Greenlaw served the whole of Scotland. There were governors and chaplains as well as guards and no doubt Greenlaw became as notorious as the infamous military glasshouse is today.

In 1849, Lieutenant Colonel Jebb CB, the inspector general, gave his report on Greenlaw. He said that, in 1848, the military district of which Greenlaw was the prison had a population of 5,103, and of the 289 prisoners, 64 were unable to read and 124 could not write, pointing to a high degree of illiteracy among the offenders at a time that most of the Scottish population were literate. Ninety, or nearly a third, were under 20 years old and 183 between 20 and 30. More than half, 154, had been in the army for two years or less, while only two had been soldiers for more than 21 years. The majority of military offenders, then, were young or very young soldiers who were not yet used to army discipline.

The nationalities are interesting with 80 English, 140 Irish and only 69 Scots. Jebb also recorded religions, with 110 Episcopalian and 124 Roman Catholic and 49 Presbyterian. The crimes were not unexpected, with 147 deserters, and 42 for absence without leave. The Army had imprisoned fifty-two for drunkenness and 16 for "disgraceful conduct," which could mean anything. Thirty-two were there for unspecified "other crimes." The governor was Captain Bristow once of the 54th Foot, and he earned £275 a year, plus free house and fuel.

Although some of the prisoners within the prison would be very unpleasant characters, the soldiers who escaped confinement were not always of a sweet and pleasant disposition either. As Kipling wrote, "single men in barracks don't grow into plaster saints." Poorly paid, harshly treated and liable to be sent to savage wars in unhealthy and primitive corners of the world, the red-coated guardians of Queen Victoria's empire were the misfits and adventurers. These were often men without hope, labourers who could not find work and youths who craved more than life in a factory or down the mines. The regiments these men joined alternated between service abroad and garrison duty within the United Kingdom.

In November 1847, the 30th Foot was based at Newcastle-upon-Tyne in northern England. Although they had the territorial designation of The Cambridgeshire Regiment, the 30th recruited from wherever the regiment happened to be situated. Many would be Irish, as the poor weather of the 1840s had severely affected the harvests of that island, forcing thousands of men to join the colours out of sheer poverty. Others were Scottish or from the terrible slums of urban England or the rookeries of old London.

In November 1847 a corporal and two private soldiers of the 30th were given charge of a prisoner and ordered to take him to the military prison at Greenlaw. One of the privates was an Edinburgh man named Campbell, with seven years' experience in the army, the other was Private Robinson, an Englishman who had been in uniform for seventeen years. The Corporal was named Walker. They had no difficulty in marching north and deposited their prisoner in Greenlaw. With their duty done, Corporal Walker asked for a pass for all three of them to spend the next day, Sunday, in Edinburgh. The officer commanding Greenlaw agreed immediately, and the three men of the 30th set off happily for the capital.

Private Campbell seems to have taken control here, introducing his companions to one of his pre-army friends a few miles outside Penicuik. After a few drams to celebrate their reunion the men of the 30th continued their journey, stopping at a public house called the Fisher's Tryst where Corporal Walker dipped into his pocket to pay for their next helping of whisky. His companions noticed that he had more in his pocket-book than might be expected, and wondered why a corporal should be so flush with money. Even after they left the Tryst, there were a few miles before they reached Edinburgh, and as the road was not yet built up, so there were many stretches without a single house in sight. About half a mile north of the Fisher's Tryst, at a desolate part of the road, Private Robinson turned on the corporal, lifted his fist and knocked him to the ground.

Taken entirely by surprise, Walker fell at once, to lie stunned on the road as Robinson took hold of his throat and held him down. Half choked, Walker looked to Campbell for help, but the Edinburgh man supported Robinson. "If you make a noise or struggle," he said, "we'll kill you."

With Campbell acting as a sentry, Robinson searched Walker's pockets. He took away the pocket-book that he had noted in the Fisher's Tryst, with its contents of £2 8/4d, as well as a pair of gloves and a very fancy silk handkerchief.

The whole affair took only a few moments and then the privates left Walker lying on the road and calmly continued their journey to Edinburgh. Either they were not the brightest of private soldiers or the whisky had taken control of their senses, for they did not attempt concealment. It was some years since Campbell had last been in Edinburgh and he did not know where to find a decent lodging house so followed the age-old advice: when in doubt ask a policeman. Meeting a police constable in Clerk Street, they asked him to recommend a suitable lodging house for the night. Always willing to help, the constable pointed them toward a respectable place in Sibbald Street.

In the meantime, Corporal Walker had recovered from the punch, the fall and its aftermath. He got up, dusted himself down and decided what to do next. Rather than seeking help, Walker immediately began a search for the two privates; after all, he was a corporal in the British Army, not some soft civilian. Jamming his hat firmly on his head, he marched into Edinburgh. As luck would have it, he met the same policeman in Clerk Street and told him what had happened. The constable listened gravely, brought him to the police office and informed the lieutenant in charge there.

"You wait here and leave this to us," the police lieutenant ordered and sent a posse of police to the Sibbald Street lodging house. Campbell and Robinson were caught by surprise and arrested without any resistance. The pocketbook with most of the money still inside, the handkerchief and the gloves were all recovered, and both men had many years to repent what had probably been a drink-fuelled moment of insanity.

Naturally, some of the prisoners were restless when confined, and in the 1850s there were a couple of arson attempts, dangerous in the timber-built prison. A gunner from the Royal Artillery tried to burn down his cell in December of 1850 and had his spell in Army detention extended by another year, and in March 1851, Robert Warner of the 13th Foot was given a year's imprisonment for "wilful fire-raising" when he also set fire to his cell.

In January 1847, some of the 76th Regiment was stationed at Greenlaw, either as temporary barracks or as guards. Three privates were on guard duty when they saw a sheep wandering in a nearby field. The temptation was too much, and within a few minutes, they had killed it and had dressed and cooked part when Constable Merrylees of the County Police found them. That must have been a compelling case for the court-martial.

In 1875, alteration work began at Greenlaw and two years later it took on the much happier role as the central brigade depot of the army in south-east Scotland. There was some drama in, January 1881, when a fire destroyed the 140-foot long, two storeys high Douglas Barracks, and the army erected a much more sensible stone building the following year. The Royal Scots took over in 1880, and in 1960 Glencorse became a training centre for Scottish infantry.

Today the army continues to garrison the fine modern Glencorse Barracks. The clock tower, once known as "the Keep" still stands from the days when Frenchmen looked at the nearby Pentland Hills and dreamed of freedom, but time has much altered the structure. The stories of the days when Glencorse echoed to French accents, or when young soldiers looked on this place with foreboding, are mostly lost, another part of Midlothian's unsung history.

Chapter 10

DANGEROUS DALKEITH

As a market and county town, Dalkeith attracted all sorts of people, farmers and farm workers, merchants and solicitors, blacksmiths and travellers. It was the hub of Midlothian, and a town with a notable history, with Cromwell's army governing Scotland from Dalkeith Castle and all the excitement of rival armies passing through in the eighteenth century. The tolbooth here was a place where justice was dispensed, and prisoners contained, while later the railway connected Dalkeith to Edinburgh and other parts of the country.

While some country places were inward-looking, Dalkeith merchants were more expansive and, in the 1750s, also owned vessels such as the 180-ton *Helen of Fisherrow* or Patrick Jackson and Company's herring buss *Buccleugh*. Dalkeith was the busy, bustling, vital centre of Midlothian where people congregated. There were ancient churches, the county court, the palatial home of the Duke of Buccleuch, rattling stage-coaches and hectic inns as well as closes crammed with the poor and lodging houses for the destitute. But such a place was a natural magnet for criminals hunting for prey, while the locals could have their disputes. The presence of the army often brought trouble as scores or hundreds of men crammed into the town looking for drink and women.

The Jacobite troubles of the eighteenth century brought both sides into the area, with Bonny Charlie's tartan-clad host marching down in their abortive attempt to replace the Germanic Georges with the autocratic Stuarts, and an incursion of government soldiers following shortly afterwards. As usual in the period, the romance of the redcoats attracted young women who yearned for a life more exciting than the mundanity of rural existence. When the reality of military life kicked in, most regretted their decision. The press carried the story of one unnamed girl from "the Neighbourhood of Dalkeith" who left her life as a servant to follow the drum in 1748. She believed that she was married to a soldier, even although he "beat and kick'd" her. She accepted the beatings as part of life, but when he called her a whore, she "took it in bad part" and returned to Dalkeith, where she committed suicide. Life was grim for many in the not-so-good-old-days.

Hanoverian soldiers seemed to have a penchant for causing trouble where women were concerned. In March 1751, there was a near riot in Dalkeith when a body of dragoons tried to kidnap a local prostitute. The Dalkeith men objected, which led to a violent confrontation with injuries on both sides with the dragoons bayonetting one local man three times.

Another flashpoint was the Dalkeith Fair, held in the broad High Street, when farmers sold animals and produce and farm servants hoped to be hired for another term. The fair also brought in the less than respectable, the pick-pockets, thieves and chancers who wished to profit at others' expense. With money passing hands and social gatherings the norm, it was expected that the pubs and change-houses should be roaring, with the nearly inevitable result of quarrels and assaults. One such happened in October 1791, when a group of drunken men attacked a journeyman wright called Henry Macmillan. It was seven at night when they picked on him, knocked him to the ground and were happily kicking lumps out of him when a local constable named William Campbell intervened. Although Macmillan was "cut and beat in a barbarous manner," he happily recovered, although without knowing the identity of his attackers. At other times, people did not have the excuse of a uniform or a fair-day to disagree; some people just did not like each other.

When Neighbours Fall Out

People often talk about the "good old days" when one could leave the door unlocked, and children played safely and happily in the streets. Those were the days of neighbourliness and community spirit. Perhaps these times did exist, but in nineteenth-century Scotland neighbours were just as likely to fall out as they are today, and when the police force was either in its infancy or non-existent, the results could be very unpleasant.

In common with many ancient Scottish towns, Dalkeith had a principal street, the High Street, while several highways passed through the town to neighbouring or distant communities. The bulk of the population lived in closes, small alleyways off the main streets that contained tenements or cottages. In one of these closes, Bennett's Close, lived James Gowans, who did not always see eye to eye with his neighbour in the same close, John Pride.

In 1825, Gowans was about forty years old, a quiet living, mild-looking man who seemed to have no quarrel with anybody. Married with three children, he was a drummer in the militia and a barber by trade. His neighbour, John Pride was an agricultural labourer, another quiet-living man with no history of aggression or violence. Unfortunately, their wives did not share the men's peaceful disposition, and their arguments and disagreements often enlivened the close. The neighbours on either side were kept awake at nights with the women screeching at each other, and the sound of raised voices was so commonplace that it became tiresome to live near Bennett's Close. Usually, the menfolk did not join in, allowing their wives to vent their spleen on each other. Nevertheless, on at least one occasion, that was not the case.

Sometime between nine and ten at night on the 20th of August 1825, John Pride returned home from working in the fields. It was early harvest time; he had been toiling since dawn, he was tired, hungry and wanted only to find something to eat and relax for an hour or so before he fell into his bed. He had not come straight home from his work, though, for he and half a dozen of his fellow labourers had stopped off at Pathhead to refresh themselves with a mutchkin of whisky. From there he had walked onto the Old Toll with a couple of companions with a further gill, then added another dram in Dalkeith itself. Pride considered that the whisky had not affected him, thought himself perfectly sober, and now he hoped for a quiet night.

However, things did not work out according to plan. Gowans was at his family home, waiting with the door open, watching outwards like a hunting spider. As soon as he saw Pride, he began to shout and swear at him, making all sorts of threats. The language, Pride claimed, was foul. Pride said nothing in retaliation, although his father-in-law, William MacMillan, who lived with them, heard the racket, opened his door and gave vent to some interesting imprecations of his own. Ann, Pride's wife, listened to both, but on this occasion, she did not join in. Perhaps she considered that her father's voice was defence enough.

Ignoring the racket, Pride went into his house and looked for food, but the cupboard was bare. Ann asked if he could go outside and find a shop where he could re-stock, and he agreed. Perhaps she did not wish to pass James Gowans in his present aggressive mood, or possibly Ann did not like to walk the dark night-time streets. Either way, as soon as Pride stepped outside his front door, Gowans was there, looming out of the gloom of the close.

"I will do for you!" The mild, slender barber said.

Before Pride could resist, Gowans lunged at him, slashing with something long and sharp. There was a tearing pain on Pride's right shoulder; he put up his hands to defend himself and gasped as something ripped at both wrists and his left hand.

"Ann!" he yelled. "Ann! Bring a light!"

Staggering away, Pride got to his front door just as Ann opened it. Her candle illuminated James Gowans as he slashed again, with the flickering yellow glow dancing from the blade of his weapon. Pride had only time for a single glance; enough to see that Gowans had fastened the blade of a razor to a pole and was poised for another stroke at him. Ann pulled her husband inside and slammed the door shut as the blood dripped onto the floor. Pride had a two-and-a-half-inch long gash on his right shoulder, lacerated wrists and a cut on his left pinkie. The Prides dared not leave the house that night in case Gowans attacked again, but one of the neighbours must have reported the disturbance as James Turnbull, Dalkeith's sheriff officer, arrived.

Turnbull searched Gowan's house and found two razors. One was tucked inside a case and was bright and clean as would be expected from a barber; the other was loose at the bottom of a chest, with its blade bent and bloodied: Turnbull was confident that was the weapon used in the assault. When the case came to the High Court in December, Gowans claimed that Pride had used threatening language and had then attacked him, but given the evidence and Pride's injuries, the jury did not believe him, and the judge ordered him to be transported for seven years. That was a bad end to a dispute between neighbours.

The question was: why? Why had the quiet Gowans suddenly snapped? Was it the result of years of tension between his wife and Mrs Pride? Or had he secretly harboured some resentment for years, and something happened that day to bring the resentment out? As in many of these cases, the motives were unclear. At least nobody was killed in that instance, which cannot be said for some other disputes between Dalkeith neighbours.

Murder in the Close

Tenement living was normal for townspeople in Scotland, as it was for much of Europe. Families and friends jostled cheek-by-jowl in vertical living, usually knowing the business of everybody else, helping out in the bad times and often squabbling about minor details and small irritations. Sometimes these minor disputes could lead to much worse troubles, as happened to a labourer named James MacKenzie on the 10th of July 1797.

As usual in such cases, there are several versions of events, with the only clear fact being the untimely death of MacKenzie. The blame was attached to another labourer named Thomas Muir, while the original cause of the dispute an argument in which neither Muir nor MacKenzie were involved.

Trying to untangle the truth from the various stories given at the High Court trial of Thomas Muir is like following the thread of a Celtic Knot in the dark while wearing gardening gloves. There is no doubt that Martha Graham, Muir's mother, and Isobel Muir, his sister, became involved in an argument with two women. One was named Montgomery MacKenzie, who was the daughter of James MacKenzie, and the other was Florence MacKenzie, who was James MacKenzie's wife.

In the trial of Thomas Muir, Montgomery MacKenzie said "a quarrel began between myself and Martha Graham about not taking her son to work." When Montgomery MacKenzie left, Martha Graham turned her ire onto James MacKenzie, and when Florence MacKenzie came to support her husband, Isobel Muir lifted a poker and whacked her across the face. Montgomery saw Thomas Muir trying to calm things down by dragging his sister and mother away, and somebody also hit Montgomery on the arm. After that, Graham and Isabel Muir returned to their own house in the close and the dispute seemed to blow over.

Later that evening, Montgomery at home was holding her child, when Graham and Isabel Muir knocked at her door. Without putting the baby down, Montgomery came forward, after which one of the other women slapped her, making Montgomery think she had hurt her child. The woman also hit Montgomery hard with a stick, "which stupefied me very much" Montgomery told the court. While she was dazed, she heard another blow but did not see it.

Montgomery's husband, John Marshall, gave a slightly different version of the story. He said when he returned from work at seven in the evening, he saw the women arguing and Isabel Muir hit his wife with the poker. After that, Thomas Muir grabbed a stick, hit Marshall over the head and struck James MacKenzie. During that excitement, Martha Graham, who had been drinking, shoved open Marshall's door and hauled out Montgomery by the hair, at the same time as Isabel Muir knocked Montgomery down with a stick. According to Marshall, at that point Thomas Muir "ran away," fetched a hammer and hit James MacKenzie over the head as he was bending over. James MacKenzie died instantly.

James MacKenzie's wife, Florence, gave a testimony that nearly matched that of John Marshall. She also said she was coming home in the evening and she "saw a mob in the close" and asked her husband what was happening. James MacKenzie told her that Martha Muir and her daughter were drunk and "were abusing him." After Isabel Muir hit her across the cheek, Florence went upstairs and the mob dissipated. After a while, Martha Graham and Isabel Muir came out of their house again and banged at Montgomery's door. Florence said she heard Montgomery cry "murder" and she ran down to help, with James in front. She said she did not see the blow that killed James.

Other witnesses added minor details, such as Alexander Wilson, who said he took the stick from Thomas Muir as he was attacking the women, a man named George Crabb tried to hold Muir back before he hit James MacKenzie and Sergeant John Wilson of the 65th Foot thought that Thomas Muir had attempted to stop his mother from causing trouble.

Thomas Muir's defence put up a different story. They said that Muir was not guilty of murder, and not even of culpable homicide as he was defending his mother from an attack at the time. The defence said that Muir had "no previous malice and he was bound by the laws of God and nature to defend" his mother "who at the time was lying on the ground and the deceased above her."

Trying to make sense of the confusing evidence, it seems that the three women were arguing, the men joined in to support their wives and things moved from verbal to physical abuse. Nobody disputed that Thomas Muir hit James MacKenzie with a hammer, although his motive was unclear. The jury found Muir not guilty of murder as the attack had not been premeditated, but guilty of culpable homicide. He was sent to the Edinburgh tolbooth and languished there for a few months before the authorities released him on the 2nd of February 1798. He had been found not guilty of murder, and could not be jailed for culpable homicide, as the prosecution had not charged him with that crime.

As well as the confusion in the closes, there were scuffles in the streets.

Footpad

The word "footpad" does not carry the same romantic overtones as "highwayman" or "pirate," but it sounds better than the modern "mugger." All these people were the same, of course: violent, dangerous thieves. Take away the romantic gloss of history and a footpad was merely a sordid, vicious criminal who caused misery for travellers on the road. The difference between a highwayman and a footpad was simple: A highwayman rode a horse to target people, while a footpad had no such luxury.

Midlothian was as much afflicted with these pests as anywhere else in Scotland, as James Taylor, a Dalkeith quarryman, found out on the 3rd of September 1836. Taylor was quietly minding his own business on the High Street, carrying a parcel of cloth for his wife, when a man named Thomas Wilson came up to speak to him. Taylor did not know Wilson well; indeed, he only knew him by his nickname of "Fittie" and had heard he could be troublesome. As Taylor had no desire to speak to Fittie Wilson, he merely asked for directions to Hare's public house, hoping that Wilson would take the hint and vanish.

No such luck. Instead, Wilson took him to Cussar's pub, where the cheap kill-me-deadly whisky rasped at the back of Taylor's throat and predatory eyes watched warily from the dark corners. Taylor and Wilson toasted each other's health in a shared gill, with Taylor grinning unhappily and Wilson allowing him to do the paying part. Uneasy in Wilson's company, Taylor tried to slide away, but Wilson followed him outside the pub and into the dark back streets, where the houses shut off the light and voices echoed from the walls of stone buildings. Taylor and Walker walked side by side, shoulders rubbing until they reached a corner where the dark was stygian, and Walker dropped all pretence of friendship.

Grabbing hold of the breast of Taylor's jacket, Wilson demanded sixpence. It seems a small sum today although to Taylor it would represent about half a day's pay. The sudden attack would also be shocking; Taylor agreed to hand the money over if Wilson took him to Hare's public house. For some reason, Wilson seemed very reluctant to enter that particular establishment and insisted that Taylor hand the money over there and then, so Taylor did so and the silver coin passed from hand to dirty hand.

Clutching the sixpence in triumph, Wilson guided his unwilling captive toward Simpson's – not Hare's - public house. There was a woman at the door by the name of Mary Bentley, and as soon as she saw Wilson, she tagged along, increasing Taylor's disquiet. He knew that any friend of Wilson's would be bad news. Wilson, however, tried to assuage his fears by saying that "Simpson's is a decent house and this woman is respectable." For some reason, possibly connected to the recent assault in the alleyway, Taylor found that hard to believe.

Finding a seat in a quiet corner, Wilson ordered a gill of whisky which Taylor kindly paid for although Wilson and Bentley did the drinking. He fumbled the money when he paid, possibly due to nerves, and rather than hand over a single sixpence, he gave Simpson two. Wilson, who must have been watching closely, said he should have the extra sixpence and offered to "count" with Taylor for it, which presumably meant some competition. However, Simpson the pub owner was having none of that and returned the coin to Taylor.

With the gill disposed of, Wilson decided they should leave, and Bentley agreed. Taylor still hoped to go to his favoured Hare's, but that seemed impossible, especially when another Mary McVicar, a woman of ill-repute joined them the moment that Wilson pushed open the door. However, Wilson agreed that Hare's public house should be their next call, as he stopped to talk to the woman.

Mary McVicar was known to the police for petty crimes, and there were vague hints of prostitution, which was immoral but not then illegal. Taylor was uncomfortable in McVicar's presence, but when he and Wilson stepped smartly along the street, he felt better as the women lagged behind and began talking together. Only when Taylor glanced behind him did he realise that the women were following. When he mentioned the fact, Wilson stopped to turn around.

"Get away!" Wilson waved an angry arm at the women. "If you follow us, I'll kick you!"

After a while, they passed William William's blacksmith's shop, and Taylor pointed out that they were on the road to Musselburgh and nowhere near Hare's house, which remark seemed to send Wilson into a frenzy. Without hesitation, he once more grabbed Taylor by the breast of his jacket, slipped a foot between his ankles and pushed him. Taylor fell, sprawled backwards on the ground and stared up in passive amazement but still managed to clutch his parcel.

"Your money or your life," Wilson said. He was obviously a man who could not create original lines. Before Taylor could move, Wilson called to the two women for help. They had not lagged far behind and now bustled up, all flowing skirts, invective and insults. As McVicar knelt on Taylor's chest, Bentley fumbled a hand inside his pocket but found that the breeches were too tight to get access. She swore and asked McVicar for a pair of scissors to cut open the pocket. Taylor must have found the next few moments nerve-wracking as Bentley cut open his breeches pocket and hauled out his money – all five shillings and two pence of it, and then took Taylor's knife for good measure. Wilson took the knife for himself. The women also grabbed the parcel Taylor was carrying, with cotton cloth, moleskin and thread for his wife.

At last Taylor showed some spirit as he wrestled an arm free and swung it back to punch at least one of his attackers.

"Take his life where he lies," Bentley advised at once, and Taylor decided not to follow through. He dropped his hand.

With Taylor's money held tightly in her hand, Bentley lifted her skirt and ran, with McVicar a few steps behind and Wilson at the rear. For all their bravery with a very docile Taylor, they lacked even the most basic common sense. They did not attempt to hide, so when a shaken Taylor informed the authorities what had happened, Wilson was picked up within an hour. Both women were in custody that same day. As there were no witnesses, it seemed that it might be a case of Taylor's word against the other three, until his knife and money were found in Wilson's pocket.

When the case came to the High Court in February, there was no doubt of the footpads' guilt. The judge transported Wilson for life, Mary Bentley for fourteen years and McVicar for seven. When the judge announced the sentences, the women lost all pretence of bravado and burst into tears. Hopefully, Taylor managed to avoid such people as he continued his quiet life.

It is easily seen that the women in Dalkeith were no shrinking violets, but were every bit as spirited as the men, and quite likely to break the law. Conversely, they could also be victims.

Murder by poison

Nobody who knew James Kid would say that he was happily married. His wife was bad-tempered, selfish, perhaps shrewish and certainly not a popular woman. The neighbours suspected that the Kids had a loveless marriage when they said the couple "did not live together as man and wife ought to do." And back in the spring of 1753, neighbours tended to notice such things in small, closed communities such as Newton, just outside Dalkeith. They also noticed that, after James Kid died in agony of some mysterious illness, his wife, Nicklas or Nicholas Cockburn was not exactly grief-stricken. She showed "no natural concern," as her neighbours said.

Nevertheless, although the neighbours thought that Nicholas Cockburn was a bit callous, nobody suspected her of foul play. Death was commonplace at the time. Two weeks later, tragedy struck again when Nicholas's father, Alexander Cockburn also died. He had worked as a forester to the Earl of Hopetoun and was on his second wife, dark-haired and handsome Susan Craig. Leaving Newton, Nicholas Cockburn travelled to her step-mother's house to assist her in preparing for her father's burial. Naturally distraught, Susan welcomed Nicholas's help, particularly as her step-daughter was willing to cook meals for them both.

On the 3rd of April 1753, Susan Craig ate a bowl of porridge and shortly after became violently ill. She experienced terrible pains in her stomach and had to retreat to her bed, where she died at five that evening.

One death was unfortunate, but two was suspicious, particularly as both of the deceased had been in good health. The authorities grabbed Nicholas Cockburn and took her before Robert Dundas of Arniston, the Lord Justice Clerk, who ordered that officials should search her house. When the searchers discovered a large quantity of arsenic, Cockburn admitted that she had mixed the poison in her husband's broth and her step-mother's porridge, and the prosecution suggested that Nicholas Cockburn had killed Craig to stop her inheriting Alexander Cockburn's money.

Female murderers were not unknown, and most killed somebody close. However, the usual victims were illegitimate children, while a woman cold-bloodedly murdering two of her closest relatives shocked even the Lord Justice Clerk. Telling Nicholas Cockburn that in other countries she could be broken on the wheel for her crimes, Dundas sentenced her to be hanged, with her body publicly dissected.

Some crimes were equally atrocious and possibly more revolting to the general population, but did not carry a capital sentence.

A scene of the most wicked lewdness

After a century of trying to stem the tide of beggars and vagrants that shambled along Scotland's highways and byways, in 1672, the Scottish Estates ordered magistrates to build houses of correction, or workhouses, where beggars could be held and encouraged to work. One of these workhouses was in Dalkeith and was known as the Charity Workhouse.

In 1758, the chaplain and schoolmaster of the workhouse was a man named James Forbes, who appeared eminently respectable to the outside world. A married man with a house at Lugtonbridge and a responsible position, Forbes must have taken care that nobody knew what happened behind closed doors. Rather than care for the children under his charge, Forbes abused them. When his wife was nursing the child of a local gentleman, Forbes took four of the young girls to his house, one at a time. As they cried and tried to fight back, Forbes slid his hands under their petticoats "upon their privy parts," and then raped them. As the *Scots Magazine* said, it was "a scene of the most wicked lewdness."

When he was brought to the court in July 1758, Forbes denied that he had "carnal knowledge" with four girls under twelve. He said it had only been three girls, not four, while his defence argued that "no law pointed out lewdness as a matter for public vengeance." Pushing the anguish of the children to one side, the defence added that rape could not be committed on girls under twelve because by law "she is incapable of consent and can have no will." When the defence tried to lower the charge to mere battery, the judge had none of it. He sentenced Forbes to be whipped through the streets of Dalkeith by the common hangman, on the 20th of August 1758, and then taken to the Tolbooth of Dalkeith for ten days. On the 30th of August, a cart would carry Forbes to Edinburgh, where he was again flogged through the streets, before being transported to the Plantations of North America for life.

Forbes was a reminder that such odious individuals have always existed. Although technology has changed, human nature has not, and crimes remain much as they have always been. Overall, Dalkeith saw its share of crimes, much like any other town of similar size.

Chapter 11

KEEP IT IN THE FAMILY

In the nineteenth century, and still today, family members commit many assaults and murders on each other. In most cases, it was a case of the physically stronger attacking the weaker, either in a drunken rage or a fit of frustration or fear. Husbands would beat wives or sons, and mothers would murder small children. Inter-family murders were so frequent that it is virtually impossible to scan a week's news in the century without coming across one or more cases of such an attack.

The number of recorded instances of wife-beating was appalling, with the police courts dealing with most cases and handing down sentences of up to sixty days. Even more tragic was the number of cases of child murder, usually by the mother. In an age where respectability was paramount and where the modern social security safety net did not exist, unmarried mothers were often treated as the pariah of society and left to cope alone with the upkeep of an illegitimate child. The combination of social stigma, poverty and post-natal depression may have been the cause for many young mothers to dispose of recently born babies. Mostly the courts were sympathetic and imposed the minimum sentence they could but occasionally the judge donned the black cap, and the mother ended her life on the gallows. Such a tragedy happened, in February 1726, when the public hangman "topped" Margaret Millar outside Dalkeith for murdering her child. That double tragedy was only one of many when family members found that circumstances were more than they could handle.

Murdering the wife

In many cases of wife or husband abuse, alcohol was a significant factor, but sometimes there were other causes. In one instance in Loanhead in 1819, early warning signs of possible trouble had been ignored. Peter Lawrie was a local man with a local job. At five in the morning of the of 22nd of December 1819, his colleague George Baillie knocked on his door to inform Lawrie that he was not going to work that day, so there was no need to wait for him.

The two were long-standing friends, so Baillie had no qualms about entering the house. Everything was normal: Lawrie was getting dressed for work while his wife, Agnes Scott, made the breakfasts and the little one was running about the floor getting in everyone's way, as small children have a habit of doing. Baillie lifted the child and kept it out of harm's way as he spoke to the parents. As usual, Lawrie was "low in spirits" but otherwise seemed quite reasonable.

Returning the child to its parents, Baillie left the house and walked homeward, only to remember something he had forgotten to say. When Baillie returned to the Lawrie's home about a quarter of an hour after his first visit, everything had changed. Agnes was lying on her bed, bleeding, and there was a fresh pool of blood on the hearth. Lawrie was sitting nearby with his head in his hands, and the child was running around, crying. Although Baillie thought she was already dead, he tried to help Agnes. After attempting to stem the blood that flowed from her head, he roused another neighbour, William Tweeddale and told him to find a doctor: Quickly. By that time, Baillie thought Lawrie looked "raised" or agitated, even though he still sat on the bed beside his wife.

When the doctor arrived, he saw immediately that Agnes Lawrie was severely hurt and decided to send her to the Royal Infirmary in Edinburgh. Ordering a cart, he bundled her on board. Baillie sat beside

Agnes on the long, jolting journey as blood seeped from a wound in her head. Baillie thought she looked too ill and tired for questions, but she did say that her Lawrie had "felled her" which was what he suspected.

Given the evidence, it was not surprising that Lawrie was arrested and charged with the murder of his wife. In the early morning of the 24th of December, George Dichmont, a sheriff officer, came to Lawrie's house, which was probably not the best Christmas present Lawrie ever had. Dichmont found him lying in bed with one of his children and took him immediately to the Calton Jail in Edinburgh. On the journey, Dichmont struck up a conversation and thought that Lawrie was sane; they spoke about Agnes, with Lawrie saying he regretted hitting her and hoped she came back to him when she recovered. Unfortunately, that was not to be. When kindly hands brought Agnes Lawrie to the care of Dr Newbigging in the Royal Infirmary, the doctor discovered that she had a severe wound on the back of her head and was delirious. Agnes never recovered sufficiently to give her side of the story and died six days later.

At Lawrie's trial at the High Court in Edinburgh, on the 14th of February, the jury listened to the possible reasons why he had attacked his wife. It seemed that he came from a family with a history of mental illness. He had an Uncle Peter who was known as "Dafty Pate Lock" while his maternal grandmother was known to be "subject to fits of despondency." According to Elizabeth Hunter, who had lived with his mother for twenty years and knew Lawrie well, he had always suffered from what she called "mental derangement" although he was never considered to be violent to anybody else.

There seemed no doubt that Lawrie was subject to bouts of depression, or "lowness of spirits" as Baillie termed it. Baillie told the court that they "made him appear not altogether right, but he could not say he was mad." He did mention an instance in the early winter when Lawrie had asked him to "come and see him hanged" which was a prediction that may well come true if the trial went against him. Other witnesses at the trial, including a paper-hanger named John Hook and a baker named John Thomson, also agreed that Lawrie was often depressed.

When Dr Renton of Penicuik appeared as a witness, he said that, in January 1819, Lawrie had typhus which made him "brain-sick" in bed for ten weeks. The aftermath was a state of "melancholy" which ended with Dr Renton's advice to go out and meet people more. Renton also said that, on one occasion, Lawrie had come to him with the story that he had lost his son to the devil and two men were coming for him. Renton believed he was a hypochondriac.

As the trial came to a climax, the defence said that three men could speak on Lawrie's behalf, but they were not available. They were all prisoners in Calton Jail, with one under sentence of transportation for sedition. After initially saying that the law barred persons in their situation from giving evidence, the judge eventually gave permission. The evidence gave further backing to Lawrie's poor mental state.

The defence did not deny that Lawrie had killed Agnes; instead, they argued that "for some time previous to, and at the period of, committing the fatal act, he laboured under mental derangement." The judge agreed. Lawrie was found guilty and sentenced to be in a mental institution for the rest of his life or until his family guaranteed he could be kept secure. It was a tragic case that highlighted the need for better medical care rather than showing any murderous intent by the killer.

Another murdered wife

Other men killed their wives without the excuse of mental illness. On the night of Monday the 2nd of September 1833, William and Fanny Gardner had been out drinking and were returning home to Bonnyrigg. Both were itinerant hawkers, which meant they walked the country going from door to door trying to entice people to buy from a basket of small goods. Although it was not a lucrative occupation, they made sufficient money to live and always had enough left over to buy a drink or three.

As there were no witnesses except William Gardner, nobody will ever know the full truth of what happened that night, but it is evident that the two fell out. Perhaps it was just a domestic dispute that went too far, or maybe drink had something to do with it, but about two hundred yards from their home, their verbal disagreement turned to physical violence. Gardner lifted his umbrella and knocked down Fanny with a terrible blow that broke the umbrella, and before she could recover he kicked her repeatedly and, apparently either stood or jumped on top of her as she lay on the ground. For some reason William could not fathom, Fanny was unable to move after that, so he dragged her home, put her on the floor and covered her with a sheet. Then, husbandly duty done, he slipped into bed for a drunken slumber.

It was after seven on the Tuesday morning when Gardner awoke, to find his wife dead. With the alcohol clearing from his system, his real feelings for her returned, and he ran to tell his neighbour, who said that Gardner had "a wildness of look." All the same, the neighbour did not believe Fanny was dead until he checked himself. With Fanny's head gashed and covered with congealed blood, and her arms heavily bruised, it was evident that there had been trouble, so the neighbour ran for help.

Two doctors, Morrison and Taylor, took Fanny away to be properly examined. Neither the wound on her head or the visible bruises had killed her, so they had a post-mortem and discovered that all her ribs were smashed, presumably where her husband had either kicked or jumped on her. Not surprisingly, Gardner was arrested and spent many years in jail.

Murdering the husband

Domestic murder was not all one-way traffic, of course. Although there were more cases of wife beating than husband beating, the latter did happen, and no doubt there were many men who were victims of emotional and verbal abuse behind the closed doors of their homes.

Sometimes a wife would use other weapons than the vitriolic savagery of her tongue, with poison one of their more common methods of killing.

In nineteenth-century Scotland, poison was frighteningly easy to obtain. A woman or man, householder or servant could quite legally buy poison across a counter with no records kept or expected, while the use of laudanum to calm the nerves, or to keep a child quiet was quite common. For murderers, poison was secret, silent, painful and deadly; women who wished to kill found it very useful, thank you for the opportunity. Of course, men could also use poison: The case of Pritchard the Glasgow-based Englishman who murdered at least two women, including his wife, is well known. However, in the nineteenth-century poison was more often seen as a woman's tool.

There were several cases where women poisoned their victims. For example, there was Mary Steel, who in October 1831 was hanged, together with her husband; Mrs Jeffrey of Carluke who murdered a man and woman, in 1838, and the well-remembered and oft-debated Madeleine Smith who may, or may not, have been a murderer. Liverpool had the infamous Black Widow murders where two sisters killed an unknown number of people, including the husband and stepdaughter of one, but Midlothian also had at least one case of death by poison.

In the nineteenth century, Midlothian was a county where the countryside juxtapositioned harmoniously with industrial towns. There were small mining communities of pits and cottages, paper mills and the central market town of Dalkeith. Amongst the bustle were some villages that, to the outside, must have appeared like rural idylls compared to the slum-ridden realities of the large cities, yet even in the most peaceful hamlet, the monster of crime crouched, waiting for a victim.

Dewartown is one of the latter. Named after the Dewar family who owned nearby Vogrie house and estate, the village consisted of a row of single-storey stone cottages that originally had turf or thatch roofs but which were later replaced with picturesque pantiles from the Vogrie brickworks. There was a range of local shops including a baker and butcher. With Pathhead a stone's throw away and only a few miles from Dalkeith, Dewartown would seem an ideal place to live. However, even here, there was discord within the family.

Peter Banks was a collier, employed by the Vogrie estate, but was a man who took out his bad temper on his second wife, Elizabeth McNeil. Such things were not rare, and in a small community such as Dewartown in the 1830s, they were hard to conceal. Old Jean Scougall and the other neighbours could not fail to hear his raised voice and possibly the sound of blows as he made Elizabeth regret her choice of husband. Eventually Elizabeth, aged about fifty and described as "a spare woman," decided that enough was enough.

One day in the spring of 1835, Jean Scougall noticed that Elizabeth had a black eye and asked her what had happened. Elizabeth proved evasive; she gave different answers each time somebody asked the question. However, at least once she said that Peter had thumped her and "he would repent it." Jean, the caring neighbour, remembered these words and later used them against Elizabeth.

At that time a mansion named Chester House was still standing not far from Dewartown. For some reason, the housekeeper, Ann McGregor, gave Elizabeth Banks a shilling out of charity. It is possible that Peter Banks kept Elizabeth short of cash as well as abusing her, but on this occasion, she had another use for the money. Rather than spending it on food or clothing, she walked to a shop in Pathhead and bought a two-penny packet of arsenic. When the shopkeeper, Mr Otto the local surgeon, casually asked why she wanted arsenic, Elizabeth told him it was to kill rats. Mrs Otto and their daughter Sarah were also present but took little interest in the transaction.

There was no argument at that; buying poison was as legal as carrying a gun, so Mr Otto handed over the arsenic without question, and Elizabeth Banks walked home and planned the murder of Peter. It was not quick, and it was not painless. Rather than kill her husband with one large dose, it seems that Elizabeth Banks mixed the arsenic with his brose, so the oatmeal and salt disguised the taste. She fed him gradually over days and watched him suffer.

Scougall saw the difference in Peter, who sickened and endured a lot of pain. Peter's son John by a previous wife also watched and, although concerned, was unable to help. However, Elizabeth must have been desperate or careless, for John also saw her openly mix "whitish powder" with the salt she sprinkled on Peter's brose. Shortly afterwards, his father had terrible stomach pains and began vomiting. When Jean Scougall asked what the matter was, Elizabeth said she thought it was cholera - which terrible, misunderstood scourge included painful stomach cramps and often ended in death. Scougall suggested that Elizabeth fetch a doctor, but Elizabeth said that her husband "would not hear" of such a thing.

When Peter eventually died, there was so much evidence against Elizabeth with her unhappy home life and the purchase of the poison that there were no other suspects. She was arrested and charged with murder. There were no visible injuries on Peter's body, but after interviewing Scougall and other neighbours, the authorities had Dr Alexander Watson perform a post-mortem. When he opened up Peter's stomach, he found sufficient arsenic to kill him, so Watson categorically stated that Peter had died of arsenic poisoning. Elizabeth appeared at the High Court in July 1835.

Despite the evidence all being circumstantial a majority of the jury found her guilty but asked for mercy that the judge was not inclined to grant. When the judge announced his sentence of death, Elizabeth showed no emotion – perhaps she expected nothing less. Her only reaction was to mutter to herself. The public hangman executed her on the 3rd of August 1835, with her hanging commemorated by a broadsheet.

There are a number of these broadsheet ballads, which are often in the form of doggerel. They were written about significant events including executions and men sold them for a penny at the scene of the execution. The broadsheet for Elizabeth was apparently written by "John McLean, Coalminer" and was entitled *Elizabeth McNeil afraid of the Hangman's Fa*.

The actual poem starts with

'Sad news I have now to tell
News of her death will gang far awa.'

One stanza paraphrases the story:

In Pathhead they ken me right well,
Guilty of that cla',
Buying doctor's arsenic pills,
To get the hangman's fa'.

There is mention of the hangman "a tricky knave, he soon my neck will draw" and of the audience, "the ladies of Edinburgh town." The broadsheet survives and is in the National Library of Scotland in Edinburgh. It is the only memorial that Elizabeth has and a sad reminder that not all marriages are blessed in Heaven.

Murdering the daughter

If there is any crime that typifies the nineteenth century, it is infanticide. It is not unique to the period of course, but the combination of several factors ensured that in that century infanticide was arguably more widespread and regarded with a peculiar horror. With a culture of respectability and a growing population, the number of unwanted pregnancies, or pregnancies out with marriage seemed to increase. Single unmarried mothers were stigmatised and often thrown out of the family home. When poverty and post-natal depression also entered the equation, it was perhaps not surprising that numbers of truly desperate women decided it was better to end the life of their child than watch it grow up in hopeless misery. However, even respectably married women could kill their own children when motherhood became a burden rather than a pleasure.

In the 1830s, Midlothian contained many small mining communities. One was at Edgehead, a village which was also known as Chesterhill. The original village sat beside the Roman road of Dere Street, adjacent to Roman Camp Hill, but it expanded when the Earl of Stair opened Edgehead Mine in nearby Windmill Woods. At its peak, the mine employed over 120 people.

One of these colliers was William Pryde, aged around forty and married to Euphemia Tait, who contemporary reports described as "swarthy" and "lank." Nothing about the Pryde family stands out; they seemed an ordinary grafting couple to the outside eye, but they did hide a family secret. Ever since childhood, Euphemia had experienced epileptic fits, which left her very depressed. At those times she became suicidal. William knew his wife and took the appropriate steps to counter her depression by hiding his razor and any other sharp objects. However, when they had a little daughter, in 1837, his precautions were not enough. Nobody will ever exactly know what happened, but one day, in April 1838, Euphemia presumably had a fit, and in the terrible aftermath she lifted her daughter and threw her out of the first-floor window.

The drop did not immediately kill the child, but her injuries were too severe for the medical treatment of the time to repair, and she died before the day was out. Rather than give Euphemia medical help, the authorities charged her with murder. Her defence argued that she was "not in a sane state of mind at the time" of the child's death, with her doctor concurring. The judge also agreed so rather than send Euphemia to the gallows, as he had the right to do, he followed his only other option and ordered her to be "kept in confinement" instead. It is a short, tragic story that perhaps epitomises one sad aspect of the period.

Killing the father

Wives, husbands, children... Every member of a family could be murdered if the conditions were right, or more accurately, wrong. Usually, it was the more vulnerable person who somebody killed, or the more unwary, but sometimes it was merely a fit of anger that decided the issue.

The Kennaways of Dalkeith were quite a close family. They had their disputes, like everybody else, patched them up and got on with the business of living. There were a great many of them, for Old John and his wife Jean McIntosh had raised eleven children between them, and what was even more telling, all eleven had survived the perils of growing into adulthood. In 1825, Old John Kennaway was 77 and had a reputation for being a "passionate man," but probably would not sire any more children. He lived with his fifty-year-old daughter Elizabeth and that day opened the door to David, his forty-year-old son. David Kennaway must have had an accident as a young man for he lived off a small pension and had just drawn out his money.

As was his wont, David visited a public house in Dalkeith and then walked along to see Old John and Elizabeth. Perhaps it was the drink, or maybe there was an argumentative streak that he inherited from his father, but David had words with Elizabeth. Words escalated to blows, and David gave her a brotherly slap that set her reeling against the wall.

Old John must have believed that the fault lay with Elizabeth for he ordered her out of the house. John hoped that his vocal son would also leave, so he would have some peace, but things did not turn out as he planned. True, Elizabeth left, but slowly, still angry and still shouting abuse at her brother. When John Kennaway reacted, by starting to his feet and grabbing a pair of fireside tongs to chase out both his offspring, David grabbed the tongs from him and dashed after his sister to continue their argument. Elizabeth turned, gave him a mouthful of passionate sisterly abuse and then ran into a neighbour's house, slamming the door in David's face before he could retaliate. She waited there for a few moments, allowing her younger brother's temper to cool down. When she heard David stomp out of her father's house, slamming the door and stamping down the stairs in a fury, she deemed it safe to return home.

Checking that her brother was indeed gone, Elizabeth pushed open the door of her father's house and stopped, shocked. Old John was lying on his back beside his bed with his nose a bloody mess and two great wounds on his forehead. His mouth and eyes were open, and his arms flung wide. He was dead, and there was no doubting who had killed him.

The sheriff officer had few questions to ask. Noting down Elizabeth's story, he interviewed the downstairs neighbours, but they could not help much. They had heard noises that they described as similar to "furniture tumbling down" and a sound like "a feather bed being dragged across the floor." Presumably, that was John falling and somebody hauling him to the bedside. The local doctor, Dr Scott, confirmed that John had died from the two wounds in his head, which left only one question: Had David killed him or did he fall onto his face in his uncontrollable rage?

When the case came to the High Court in December 1825, the jury had no difficulty in deciding that David had struck the fatal blows. They found him guilty of culpable homicide, and the judge transported him for life to Bermuda.

Assaulting the Mother

Ann Baillie was a bad-tempered, drunken woman, who spent her time between the public houses and the cheap lodging houses of Dalkeith. Sometimes she spoke to her mother, sometimes, she did not. On Sunday the 11th of August 1844 the two women were in a lodging house and Ann, drunk as usual, ordered her mother to buy some tobacco for her pipe. Her mother said she would go if Ann provided her the money. That simple request sent Ann over the edge, and she punched her mother, who fell to the ground and immediately went into an epileptic fit. That did not deter Ann, however, who continued to kick her as she lay there. The mother died early the following morning, and Sergeant McPherson of the County Police arrested Ann.

Was that murder? Or was it culpable homicide? Or did the mother die because of her fit? The jury thought it was culpable homicide, but the case only serves to show how easy it is to kill somebody. One second of uncontrolled anger is all it takes. It is a sobering realisation to know how fragile our lives are.

Chapter 12

ROBBERY IN DALKEITH

There has always been theft and robbery. Temptation, the desire to own something, jealousy of somebody else's possessions, greed, hunger or just plain badness have all driven people to steal since time began. Occasionally, there were touches of black humour, such as a robbery in the stables of Masterton Mains by Newbattle. Although the farm servants lived in the stables, on the evening of the 28th July 1823, a thief broke in and stole the clothes of the sleeping men, as well as a silver watch. In return, the thief left his own, sadly battered, jacket.

Farmhouses could be locked and bolted, with shutters securely fastened and any valuables hidden away, but the outbuildings, with rudimentary protection or none at all, were easy targets for the thief. The farmers, of course, tried to fight back as best they could, such as in the summer of 1762 when the charmingly named "Society of Farmers for Prosecuting Rogues" met in Dalkeith. The Society offered a reward of five guineas – a huge sum by the standards of the time – to anybody who helped find the thief who had been stealing "plough irons, harrows and utensils for labouring."

By the nineteenth century, the forces of law and order were more organised, and sometimes the police could get lucky, or perhaps they just used their experience to sniff out wrongdoers.

On Friday the 19th April 1844, Sergeant McPherson of Dalkeith learned that somebody had stolen some shirts from Millerhill. It was a typical minor rural crime that would never make the headlines, so he took note and continued with the routine of the day, probably never expecting to hear any more about it. However, the next day, about noon, he was on patrol between Sheriffhall and Millerhill when he saw two young men coming toward him. They were of the age that then was known as "lads"' and today would be "youths", that awkward, no-longer-boys-but-not-yet-men stage in which young males are either overly brash or are not sure how to act or what to do. As soon as they saw McPherson, the lads turned away, which naturally aroused the policeman's suspicions.

Chasing after them, McPherson recognised the lads as George Thomson and William Hart, both recently released from prison for theft. When he caught them, he asked awkward questions, and they confessed they had been busy selling shirts at a pawnbroker and had others at their lodgings. Some were indeed from the theft at Millerhill and others from a break-in at Lugton of which McPherson had not yet learned. With the shirts recovered, both young men were soon back in prison, where they probably belonged.

These may sound like minor crimes, and although murders always make the headlines, ordinary people were much more likely to be the victims of less vicious but still upsetting offences. Drunken assaults and petty theft were the norm, but for property owners or shopkeepers, there was always the possibility of a robbery that could destroy a business and alter comfortable security to near poverty in the course of one night.

Shopkeepers, particularly those whose premises held valuable stock, took every possible precaution to keep burglars out, and the law had some pretty harsh penalties to deter the criminal classes. Even so, there were professionals who spent their lives breaking into securely locked premises to steal what they could.

There were many methods by which burglars could rob houses, shops or offices. Many cracksmen, as the most expert burglars, were known, used a small boy to crawl through a skylight or fanlight, or even to squeeze between the iron bars of a downstairs window. This boy, whose "cant" name – cant was the unofficial slang of the criminal classes - was a "snakesman", would either open the nearest window or unbolt a door for the adult to enter. Other cracksmen would opt for bribery and friendship, becoming close to a crooked servant who would leave a door or window open. In the census of 1851, around seven per cent of the population were servants; there were twice as many women working in service as employed in mills or factories. The nineteenth century was an age of mobility, with servants seldom staying in the same household for long, so there was not always loyalty to what was a temporary employer. Added to that were the low wages most servants suffered and the often-poor working conditions where a bitter-tongued mistress could create resentment in an ill-used girl. Servants could repay such abuse by passing on information about the contents of her mistress's house to a friendly cracksman, or screwsman, if, the burglar used a key rather than other methods of entering.

Other criminal methods were more unpredictable, such as the thief calling at the house in the guise of a peddler, sending the servant to find the mistress and stepping inside the house for a quick scan to see what was inside, or acting the sneak thief and grabbing what was close to hand. However, there were also genuinely expert cracksmen who relied on tools to break in. These could be improvised from the conventional tradesman's tools or ordered from craftsmen who specialised in making equipment for burglars. Despite its reputation for shoddy "Brummagem" work, Birmingham was the centre of this criminal trade.

There were many types of lock-picks that an expert could utilise to unfasten even the most reluctant door in seconds. Bars on windows were no defence: Cracksmen could pull them apart by the use of a doubled cable and a steel rod, loop the cord around two bars and the rod, then twist the rod to exert sufficient pressure to bend one of the bars. There were also specialised jacks to push bars apart. A good cracksman could defeat shutters by using a brace-and-bit to bore a hole and then reaching inside to open the bar that closed them. He could use a glass-cutter's stone to cut window glass, or he could scrape away the putty around an entire pane. In a quiet street, the cracksman would use a jemmy to lever open a door or a safe. There was no end to the ingenuity of a cracksman if there was a crib to crack and loot to be had. Even easier, many burglars could use false or skeleton keys. They would "borrow" a servant's key, take a quick wax impression, or press it into putty or even chalk and have a copy made in some shady back street workshop.

In Scotland, it was quite common for thieves to enter the flat above a shop, cut through the floor and drop a knotted rope or even a rope ladder to the floor below. One enterprising Edinburgh thief got clean away with an excellent haul of jewellery by this method until a police constable who had been in the Navy noticed the seaman-like knots of the rope ladder and cast about for a local nautical thief. At other times, the burglar could enter the cellar of the house or shop next door, tunnel through the adjacent wall and work upward. A shopkeeper had to prepare him or herself for assault from every angle.

Inside information was essential. The professional cracksman could watch his target for days or weeks to work out the movements of the residents. People of regular habits were easier to rob; for example, a family who went to church on a Sunday, and insisted that the servants joined them, was asking for a thief to visit during the times of church service. The robbery of the Greenock bank, in 1828, had been months in the planning, with the cracksmen travelling from London to Greenock as early as June the previous year to begin their observations and work out when the bankers were absent.

The best cracksmen were international, but these were few and far between. There were more who travelled within the British Isles, arriving in a town or city to work on a particular "job" and leaving immediately after.

People may not immediately think of Scotland as a target for international cracksmen, but throughout the nineteenth century, there were many high-profile robberies in the country. The Argyll Arcade and some hotels in Glasgow and Edinburgh's jewellery shops were all targeted at various times, while even Midlothian, seemingly beneath the main criminal horizon, was not immune.

William Robertson ran a high-quality shop in Dalkeith High Street, selling fabric of different types and some jewellery, mainly watches. He knew that if a cracksman targeted any shop in Dalkeith, it would be his, so he took stringent precautions to keep the burglars out. The shop had two doors, an outer and an inner, with the inner door having a double lock, and at night, Robertson set a guard dog loose in the shop. If anybody entered, the barking of the dog would alert him or his wife. As he lived in the flat above the shop, nobody could get access through the ceiling, and there was no basement or cellar to allow subterranean tunnelling.

As was their habit, on the night of the 31st October 1809, Mrs Christian Robertson and John Colcleuch, the apprentice, had been in the shop. At half-past eight, they shut and locked the doors, as always, checked them and while Colcleuch went home, Christian carried the shop keys upstairs. She put the keys in their drawer and locked that as well, so there was no possibility that the thief could use the shop-keys to gain access. At about eleven, William said it was time to put the dog in the shop, as he always did, so Christian handed him the keys and he went downstairs.

He came back almost immediately, distraught because both the back doors were unlocked and swinging open. Somebody had robbed the shop.

The burglar or burglars chose the time that the Robertsons had closed the shop and had not yet put in the guard-dog. There was no doubt that the burglar knew his business: He was a skilled screwsman rather than a casual blunderer. If he had forced the doors, the noise would have alerted the Robertsons in the flat above, so the burglar used a false key. He must have been watching the shop for some days to learn the Robertsons' routine.

As soon as William gave her the news, Christian joined him downstairs, and together, they checked the stock. The watch case had been picked and lay open, and some parcels of cloth had been lifted from the shelves while others lay open on the counter. The thief had got away with ten silver watches, a pound sterling in silver change and a great deal of valuable cloth, including two pieces of superfine black fabric, black silk Florentine and French cambric. Overall, the thief stole stock valued at over £200. That does not sound a great deal in the twenty-first century, but in 1809, a skilled workman would be lucky to earn a pound a week, and a servant may pocket only five pounds a year.

No doubt upset, perhaps trembling, William checked the door to see if the lock still worked or if it was broken. He found it difficult to turn the key, which was unusual, but the lock still functioned. There was no sign of forced entry, so the burglar had undoubtedly used a false key rather than a jemmy. Not only that, but the burglars must have been aware that William would not have been back in the shop until eleven, for rather than grab anything they could and run, they knew they had time to select only the best. There were several parcels of less valuable material that had been opened and rejected.

William Robertson knew he had to act fast. He realised that the robbery must have taken place only an hour or so earlier so the thief, or thieves, may still be close. William immediately woke Colcleuch, told him what had happened, and the two of them ran to the sheriff officer for help. The sheriff officer knew the habits of most thieves in Dalkeith and suggested they tour the public houses first. He would know the area and would recognise any known thieves, but in the event, they had no luck that way. The pubs were quiet and law-abiding that Tuesday night.

While the Robertsons and Colcleuch returned to bed, if not to sleep, the sheriff officer continued his investigations. He thought it evident that there was more than one thief, for it would take a strong man to carry away such a quantity of material. It was also obvious that the thief would try to sell the cloth and watches somewhere. As people in Dalkeith would soon learn of the robbery and be alert for stolen goods, the thief would probably travel to Edinburgh to find a fence to take the goods.

The sheriff officer began to question people who had travelled on the road between Dalkeith and Edinburgh. He found a couple of individuals who might have helped him build a case. One was William Mackintosh, who worked as a clerk at the legal firm of James Smith and was walking to Dalkeith when he found a piece of cloth lying on the road. Mackintosh picked the cloth up but handed it over the sheriff officer told him it might have been stolen. Even more significantly, Mackintosh also saw two men walking toward Edinburgh with large "bundles on their backs." That made the sheriff officer think he was going in the right direction, so he was pleased when he spoke to an Edinburgh servant, named Margaret Cochran, who had found a length of cloth on the street in St Patrick's Square in Edinburgh.

It seemed that there were two men involved, that they had taken so much material that they dropped some and they had gone to the St Patrick Square area of Edinburgh.

The sheriff officer elicited the help of James Wilson, Sheriff Clerk in Edinburgh, who knew the city well. Wilson did the usual rounds of the pawn shops and lodging houses and was soon talking to somebody with an interesting story. Janet Patison was a servant in a lodging house in Crosscauseway, no distance at all from St Patrick Square. She had a trio of lodgers in the garret: A man and wife who claimed that their name was Smith, and a man named Brown. The very commonality of the names must have sounded suspicious to Wilson. The three had come to the lodgings about the middle of October, two weeks before the robbery.

When Wilson asked if she had noticed anything unusual about these lodgers on the night of the 31st, Patison became quite agitated. On that night, Mr Smith was away from the lodgings, leaving his wife with Mr Brown, which Patison thought a bit strange in itself. Mr Smith came back to the house at seven in the morning, knocking at the door in a bit of a state. He seemed annoyed that the door was bolted, which Patison explained was standard practice to keep out the thieves and nightprowlers, and she noticed that Smith's shoes and stockings were all dusty as if he had been walking. Patison said Smith looked "haggard" and she was sure he had been out all night. As soon as Patison drew the bolt and opened the door, Mr Smith ran past her without speaking a word. The sheriff clerk took note of all that Patison said.

As usual in such cases, the authorities had a good idea who the lawbreakers were and where such people spent their time. There was also a network of informers ready to divulge titbits of information about strangers or people who were less than honest. Either an informer advised them, or they knew where to go, for Wilson asked Alexander Callander, a town clerk, and other officials to accompany him when he walked into John Milne's change house (public house) in Infirmary Street, a brisk five-minute walk from Crosscauseway. As they arrived, Mr and Mrs Smith decided it was time to make a quick exit; they recognised the forces of the Law. Seeing the Smiths bolt from the change house, a town officer named Archibald Campbell sprang forward and grabbed hold of Smith, who immediately dropped a silver watch on the ground.

As the scene attracted a crowd that might have turned hostile, Wilson thought it best to take the Smiths back inside the change house and out of public view. He searched Smith and found another two silver watches in his waistcoat pocket, a knife and five shillings in change. When she saw her husband's guilt proved, Mrs Smith burst out crying and ran to the kitchen, shouting to Mary Wilson, the servant to hide her as officers were chasing her. As Mary Wilson watched, bemused, Mrs Smith moved quickly to a wooden bench, plumped herself down and refused to co-operate when the officers entered. She sat there, solid, crying, with her arms folded and her feet firmly on the floor. Only when the officers forcibly removed Mrs Smith did Wilson find two cards of lace and a cutting of silk underneath the bench. Mary Wilson was confident they had not been there before: This was an Edinburgh change-house, not a fabric dealer's shop.

With the Smiths safely in custody, Wilson led a posse of officers to their lodgings in Crosscauseway. They arrested Brown right away and rummaged the garret for stolen goods. There was little of interest in the room itself, but on the slate roof outside, there was a silk vest and a bale of superfine cloth, while a closet in the house yielded another bundle of fabric. There was no practical reason to store such a valuable item on a rooftop in a Scottish winter, so the case seemed proved.

When the officers questioned him, Smith had a story ready. He was an Englishman - his accent made that obvious – and he said his stay in Edinburgh was only temporary. Smith said he was lodging with Brown only until some money arrived from friends in England, and then he intended to return south. When asked about the watches and the material, Smith said that a chapman in Leith had offered him the lot for £13 and he had beaten him down to only £8. Naturally, he did not remember the chapman's name: Does one ever know the name of travelling peddlers? Smith claimed he had also bought a cloth coat from an auction room somewhere in the Bridges. And as for Janet Patison's story, well, the woman must have been mistaken: He had been in his lodgings all night, warmly tucked up in bed.

Doubting Smith's story but willing to give the benefit of the doubt, Wilson ordered a clerk named Alexander Patterson and another officer to escort him to the house in Leith where he claimed to have met the packman. As they walked down Leith Walk, Smith broke free and made a run for it, and there were a few frantic minutes when he scampered down the street with the two sheriff's clerks racing after him. The clerks must have been experienced at their job for they grabbed his collar and held on tightly as he struggled and yelled for help that was not forthcoming.

With his escape bid foiled, Smith seemed to try and co-operate but was unable to remember where he met the chapman. He did eventually knock at the door of a vintner - wine merchant - named Cumming in St Bernard Street, but Cumming denied ever having seen him before. The search for the shop where he bought the coat was equally elusive.

Now came an important discovery that Wilson probably already guessed. Smith had used a false name; his real name was John Armstrong, and he was a known professional burglar. At one time, of course, the Border Armstrongs had been famous reivers, outlaws wild men and general do-badders, so John Armstrong was merely following a family tradition. He had been accused of involvement in a significant burglary at the packing hall of Hutcheson and Son of Montrose Street in Glasgow the previous year, but the trial jury found him not proven. However, the jury had found his co-accused, George Stewart and John Gordon McIntosh guilty of stealing 104 pieces of printed calico cloth. Both men were hanged that November. Foolishly, Armstrong had not learned and quickly returned to his old thieving ways.

Armstrong's trial took place at the High Court on the 14th December 1809. He pleaded not guilty, but with so much evidence against him, he was not so lucky this time and was condemned to be hanged in Edinburgh on the 17th January 1810. Robbery did not always pay.

Chapter 13

SURVIVING THE HIGHWAYS

Until the advent of proper police forces, the highways and byways of Scotland could be perilous places. With a smaller population than now, and before the agricultural revolution had improved the landscape, there were many lonely stretches between settlements where highwaymen or footpads could strike. The environs of a major city were always dangerous, for highwaymen were acutely aware that they had better opportunities for affluent customers on busy roads. Other favoured areas for highwaymen were routes leading from markets and fairs, where farmers could have sold their produce or animals and may have indulged in a little refreshment before returning home. Such men, flush with cash and filled with good cheer, may not have been sufficiently wary.

Mention the word highwaymen, and the mind often brings up an image of a masked desperado, a daring rogue who was gallant to ladies, brave in the face of danger and willing to face the gallows. He robbed the rich, took a drink on the way to execution and joked that he would pay on his return. He would ride a fine horse, gallop up to a coach and four, present his pistol to the driver and demand that he halt so that the passengers can "stand and deliver", often with the obligatory "your money or your life." The highwayman is something of a figure of romance, a picture of daring, with the legendary Dick Turpin arguably the best known of all.

The reality, of course, is quite different. Highwaymen were neither romantic nor daring; they were sordid thieves who often targeted vulnerable travellers on lonely stretches of road, spreading fear and robbing people of their livelihood, before running away to hide. Although English highwaymen have had most of the publicity, Scotland also had her share of such unpleasant characters, with Midlothian a happy hunting ground. Sometimes, the area around Dalkeith seemed to be infested with highwaymen, particularly during the time of agricultural fairs. There were periods of relative quiet on the roads, and times when it seemed that highwaymen were queuing up to rob innocent travellers. Crime often increased after a war when soldiers were paid off. After years in the army, men, often brutalised by war and with no skills other than killing, took to robbery to live. At other times, soldiers did not wait for the outbreak of peace before they became a menace to the general public.

On the late evening of Tuesday 13th March 1736, William Gladstanes of Simmiestown was walking into Edinburgh from Penicuik. He was near the gibbet at Newington, that constant reminder of the fate of wrong-doers when five people approached him. Gladstanes noticed that one was a woman, two he could hardly see in the dark, and the other two he saw wore military scarlet. Before Gladstanes could say anything, the soldiers drew their bayonets, and all five attacked him. Gladstanes had little chance to escape as the mob beat him up and robbed him of £17 and his personal papers. That was a typical attack on the highway, short, brutal and ugly, with neither romance nor glamour.

Not all attacks were successful, such as the footpad who attacked a gentleman near Edmonston outside Dalkeith, in August 1743. The would-be robber presented a pistol and pressed the trigger, but the ball missed, the traveller kicked in his spurs and galloped past without any ill effects except a bit of a scare.

The thieves were not always after silver and gold. At a time when most people lived on the edge of poverty, anything that could sell was welcome. Such was the case in the summer of 1749, when James Griffin and William Watson robbed James and Thomas Carr, carriers on the "King's High Road near Dalkeith" according to the *Newcastle Courant*. After all the trouble of arranging a robbery, all they took was twelve pieces of "Scots Holland" cloth and "some woollen stuff" before they ran south. Both were captured in Northumberland and ended in jail in Morpeth.

Carriers and carters were a prime target for such petty theft. In December 1772, John Donaldson, a carter who operated between Dalkeith and Edinburgh, was passing the then-hamlet of Bridgend near the Inch, south of Edinburgh when Daniel McLeish, the gardener, invited him in for a drink. As carting was thirsty work, Donaldson pulled his cart to a stop and happily jumped off. However, while Donaldson refreshed himself, ably assisted by McLeish's wife, Janet Fouler, McLeish was helping himself to items from the cart.

When Donaldson realised he had pieces of table linen missing, he informed the authorities, detailing his movements. It was not hard to work out where the goods had been lost, and soon McLeish and Fouler stood before the bench. When the prosecution pointed out the sheriff officer had found the missing linen hidden at the bottom of a chest in McLeish's house, the case was proven. The judge sentenced McLeish to be whipped through the streets of Dalkeith and then banned him and Fouler from Midlothian for life. Other thieves were more traditional and straightforward in their get-me-rich schemes.

During the cold winter of 1766 to 1767, one particular highwayman haunted the highway between Dalkeith and Edinburgh. Dressed in striped clothes, he held up travellers with his pistol and then vanished. In the first week of January, this highwayman ambushed the Edinburgh wagon as it rumbled from Dalkeith to the capital. Showing no interest in the goods in the wagon, the thief took all the cash from the driver before galloping away into the rain. It seems he worked without an accomplice and robbed a pair of gentlemen near Dalkeith a few days later. Unlike most highwaymen, he seems to have escaped scot-free.

Highwaymen preferred the long nights of winter where, in the days before street lighting and when carriages had only a couple of faint lanterns to enable them to view the road ahead, a rider could loom out of the dark unseen and unheard. It is hard to imagine the darkness of these days when people in the country went to bed early, and the only lighting was candles, crusie lamps or whale-oil lanterns. The moon was a godsend, ghosting its light over a countryside where many farms remained unenclosed, people huddled in tight communities of often-thatched cottages, and the weather dictated travel conditions. Snow closed roads, carriages toppled on windy days or slewed sideways in the deep ruts of muddy roads and people peered into the dark in fear of wandering bands of gypsies, idle beggars or the sorners – professional thieves that travelled the countryside, targeting isolated communities. Occasionally there were attacks whose motives remain a mystery.

On the 20th October 1767, Adam Conquergood was returning to Edinburgh from Dalkeith Fair. Conquergood was an Edinburgh man, a shopkeeper from the West Bow, a steep, heavily curved street that ran from the High Street down to the Grassmarket. He was in a good mood, he had sold a horse at the fair, and the money was heavy in his pocket. At about eight o'clock, Conquergood was riding past Edmonston Park Dyke when a man on foot appeared from out of the gloom. Surprised, Conquergood glanced at him, and the man grabbed the bridle of his horse, snarling at him to stop. Before the shopkeeper could respond, the highwayman fired a pistol.

The ball crashed right through Conquergood's hand and hit him in the chest, an inch or so above his heart. Probably in shock, Conquergood dismounted and told his attacker that he could have his money, but asked him not to kill him. Strangely, after apparently achieving his objective, the highwaymen ran away without stealing a thing. When a group of people appeared from the darkness behind, the highwayman jumped back over the dyke.

Wounded and in pain, Conquergood could only lead his horse along the dark road until he came to a weaver's house. Staggering inside, he collapsed, and the good people made him as comfortable as they could while they sent for a doctor. As the ball was right under the breastbone, the doctors thought it safer to leave it where it was rather than extracting it, and then the questions began.

Why had the highwayman attacked him without demanding money? Had it been a personal attack rather than a mere robbery? Was there something hidden in Conquergood's past? After a while, the questions began to upset Conquergood, and he stated that he would take anybody to court if they challenged his character. The motivation for that attack is not known, but plenty other highwaymen were infesting the roads of Midlothian.

Not all highwaymen were successful. In the early days of December 1772, two men ambushed the chaise of a lady as she travelled into Dalkeith. The driver pulled up at the threat of a pistol, but when one of the men tried to open the chaise door, he whipped up the horses and galloped away, leaving the would-be robbers impotent and no doubt cursing at the side of the road.

In the early nineteenth century, the Scottish countryside still had a massive influence on the capital city. There was the Grassmarket just beneath Edinburgh Castle where farmers hired labourers, sheep grazed on the slopes of Arthur's Seat – and would do until the latter half of the twentieth century - and the suburbs of Stockbridge and Newington lapped onto fields. So it was not unusual that James Hunter of Edinburgh's St Leonard's Street should be a cowfeeder and spend much of his time working outside the city.

On Tuesday the 18th April 1826, Hunter had been successful at Lauder Fair, so he was careful of the £10 -17 shillings and sixpence that he had in his possession when he began the long walk back to Edinburgh. He rolled the coins up in his eleven bank notes: seven were guinea notes, each one worth one pound and one shilling, and one of these was from the Renfrewshire Bank.

At that time, people thought nothing of walking distances that would make the modern pedestrian wince. A five-mile walk to work was nothing before a ten-hour day and walking between Lauder Market and his home was just routine for Hunter. Before he left Lauder,

Hunter bought some refreshment to fortify him for the journey, so he was slightly elevated as he left the town at around two in the afternoon.

It was about seven when he ascended the steep side of Soutra Hill, with the evening light soft across the heather slopes and the view unravelling across the entire Lothian plain, the Firth of Forth and over to the grey-blue hills of Fife in the far distance. As he crested Soutra, two young women greeted him with friendly waves and big smiles. They were Mary Somerville and Elizabeth Lawrie; they had also been at Lauder Fair and were walking back to Edinburgh. Whoever said that nineteenth-century women were scared and meek had not met these two, walking across Scotland to go to a fair, and then walking back home again.

The women joined Hunter, for companionship was always welcome on the lonely roads, particularly as night was gathering and there were still many miles to cover before they reached Edinburgh. As the darkness increased, a rising moon cast a silver gloss across the fields, lighting their path. At ten at night, they arrived at Dalkeith, with the moon now full and free of clouds; the road was clear before them.

At about midnight as they neared Craigover Brae, about three miles south of Edinburgh, three men joined them. Hunter thought they might be coal carters, but he was not sure. They wore jackets and trousers, rather than breeches, and he noticed that the jacket of at least one of them was either new corduroy or perhaps velveteen. The men walked with them for a couple of hundred yards and then dropped behind. As they crested Craigover Brae, one of the men ran up and punched Hunter behind his left ear, tripped him, grabbed his collar and hauled him backwards, so he stumbled and fell, face up on the ground.

Hunter rolled over and lay on his right side, trying to protect the notes in his pocket. He had only time to shout "Murder" once before the attacker stifled his cries with a rough hand, and then pressed his head hard against the ground so he could not look up and see what was happening. Mary Somerville had seen enough; she grabbed hold of Hunter's attacker and tried to pull him away, but the second man turned on her, lashed out and threatened to knock her down unless she got out of his way.

Sensibly, the women did not linger. There was a house about fifty yards down the road at the foot of the brae, and Somerville lifted her skirt and fled there, banging on the door for help. There was no answer; she stood on the outside of a locked door at midnight, while three violent men robbed an innocent cowfeeder within shouting distance.

As Hunter lay there, a second man stood over him while the third hung back and did not become involved, either to help or to attack. The two men knelt on him, pressing him down with their knees as they delved into the left pocket of his breeches and pulled out some of his silver, although for some reason they left him with five shillings and sixpence.

"Turn over!" The first man ordered, but Hunter refused, so the man told his companion to turn him around as he "certainly has more money." At that point, Hunter heard the man holding his head called "Jamie" and tucked the information away, aware he could use it later.

The footpads then roughly yanked him around and dipped into his right pocket, taking away all his notes. Not yet satisfied, one said:

"Loose the napkin, and we will get the bastard more easily choked."

As the man Jamie loosened the grip on his mouth, Hunter begged them to:

"Leave some life in me" as for a moment he thought his attackers would murder him. However, they only untied his neckcloth and ripped it away, with the man called Jamie taking his umbrella before both men hurried away. Immediately the men left, Hunter tried to rise, but Jamie was still within earshot, returned at once and smashed him back to the ground while the second man watched, then stepped contemptuously across Hunter's prostrate body.

Hunter thought it wise to lie still until he was sure his attackers were gone. He watched them walk southward on the road for a few hundred yards before going into the fields and out of his sight. Struggling to his feet, Hunter followed, angry now and determined not to let his attackers get away scot-free. He plunged into the field behind them, scrambled over a dry-stane dyke to the next field and suddenly realised that he was alone and hurt, chasing three desperate men into a very lonely place at night. His sense told him that self-preservation was more important than money, and he returned, frustrated, to the road.

The two women were already there, together with the male occupant of the house, who had eventually succumbed to their persistence and come to help. Mary was shocked at Hunter's appearance, with blood smearing his face, his eyes wild and his neck bare to the elements.

Shaken and angry, Hunter lost no time in informing the sheriff officers what had happened and they began their enquiries. There was a recognised procedure in such matters. If it was a case of theft, get a description and tour the pawn shops and then the pubs to see if the item was for sale. If it was an assault or robbery, then visit the public houses and inns looking for men or women who may fit the description of the attackers and who may suddenly be spending more money than they should. It was a simple method, but most of the time, it was surprisingly successful.

The sheriff officers noted the description of the attackers: Three men dressed like coal carters in jackets and trousers, one perhaps in velveteen and possibly flashing around banknotes. Mary Somerville added her two-pence worth when she said that one man, Jamie, had a dark complexion. It was not much to go on in an area where there were many coal carters wearing jackets and trousers, but it was better than nothing.

The first place they tried was David Finlayson's spirit shop at Edmonstone, which was around a mile away from Craigover Brae. With no opening time regulations, pubs opened all hours, and Finlayson said that his shop had been busy that day, but he checked his takings to remind him. Most men would pay with copper or silver, but one customer had parted with a twenty-shilling note, which meant Finlayson had to give him a great deal of change. There had been three in that party, he remembered, and they bought two half mutchkins of whisky.

The sheriff officer found that very interesting and asked Finlayson: "Could you describe these men?"

"I can do better than that," Finlayson said as the memories returned; "I can name them. They were James Renton, although most folks call him Jamie, Andrew Fullarton and a fellow called Reid." He explained the sequence of events.

Four men, including Renton and Reid, came into Finlayson's shop at about five in the evening the day of the Lauder Fair. Fullerton joined them sometime after eight, and they remained, drinking, until quarter to twelve when they all left, apparently to go to Fullerton's aunt. About an hour later, Renton, Fullerton and Reid returned and remained until sometime after four the next morning. It was on this second visit that they paid with the banknote.

Interested in the story, the sheriff officers continued their investigations as they pieced together the wanderings of what were now their three chief suspects. From Finlayson's, the three men had found their way to Cosser's hostelry in Dalkeith, into which they staggered at half past six the day after the fair. They asked for a half-mutchkin of whisky and paid with a guinea note, which was not welcome at that time of the morning as it was hard to find sufficient change. James McCarter, who served them, said they had "the look of men who had not got any sleep the previous night."

The three men asked McCarter if a stagecoach was leaving for Edinburgh that day and when they learned there was not, they made vague enquiries about hiring a post-chaise. Either the price put them off, or they were merely casting a red herring for they did not hire the chaise but left that inn and walked away, southward, the opposite direction from Edinburgh.

The sheriff officer nodded and left the inn. He was not entirely convinced that the three could have walked far in their exhausted and half-drunken state, so he continued his enquiries locally. He found that they next stopped at the public house of James Drummond, still in Dalkeith. Drummond knew Fullerton by sight but not the other two men, whom the officer presumed to be Renton and Reid. Drummond thought they looked "much fatigued" as they asked if Mrs Drummond was out of bed yet as they wanted breakfast. Drummond asked if they had visited Lawrie's Den, which was an inn on Soutra and the three agreed that they had passed it in the dark, which suggests they were pretending they had walked in from Lauder Fair.

Moving on in a probably increasingly erratic fashion, the three next called at another public house in Dalkeith where a man named Robertson said they bought one shilling and tenpence worth of whisky and handed over a pound note of the Renfrew Bank. Robertson refused that note but accepted one from the Sir William Forbes bank instead. The three met Alexander Finlayson in that establishment. He was a carter with a load of stones for an address in Dalkeith, but he willingly stopped to share a couple of half mutchkins of whisky and a glass of beer. He did not pay, and the idea of him parting with banknotes seemed to be amusing. Where the devil would a carter get a banknote from? Robertson seemed to suggest.

Having followed the trail of the suspects and proved their possession of a variety of banknotes, the sheriff officer only had to see if they had any other sources from where they could have obtained the money they spent so freely. The wages they earned were never above a pound a week, so they would not have bank notes. There was no doubt in the officer's mind: These were his men. Calling up reinforcements, he pounced and arrested Renton and Fullarton. He was less successful with Reid, who had fled.

The trial of Renton and Fullarton took place at Edinburgh's High Court in July 1826. Given the evidence, there was no surprise when the jury found James "Jamie" Fullarton, guilty. When the judge sentenced him to be hanged on 16th August, he began to weep. The jury found the case against Renton not proven, and he walked free but carrying a shadow of doubt that would follow him all his life. Reid remained free.

Joseph Gibson: Highwayman

Of Midlothian's share of highway robbers, none even remotely aspired to the romantic category. Joseph Gibson was typical of their sordid careers; his star rose quickly, flared briefly and fell into spectacular darkness. How many people even know his name today? Probably only a handful, and then with a couple of fingers spare.

James Martin, a carter who worked for Peter Cathie and Company, Fisherrow wood merchants, was one of the first to meet Gibson the highwayman. That was on the night of 10th October 1812, when the autumn wind whipped the few remaining leaves from the trees and drove occasional bursts of chilling rain against Martin's face. He was riding one empty cart and leading another on the road northward from Biggar to Musselburgh and had just passed Wanton Walls, with Niddrie looming up when a man came up to him.

"It's a fine night," the man spoke in a soft Irish accent.

"Very fine," Martin replied cheerfully, glad of the company.

Although it was late, sometime between eleven o clock and midnight, there was enough of a moon for Martin to see that the man wore a uniform. That was not unusual at a time that Britain had been at war almost continuously since 1793 and the country was full of sailors, soldiers, yeomanry and militia. Martin saw that this man wore a light blue jacket and a foraging cap, with the white trousers of a soldier.

"Are you heading toward Musselburgh?" Martin asked. The soldier said that he was and lagged behind. He drew something from under his tunic; Martin thought it might be a pistol but was not sure.

"Stop!"

The soldier gave the order as he stepped forward. Still sitting on the right side of the leading cart, Martin looked at the man as he approached from the left side of the cart.

"Why should I stop?" Martin asked.

The soldier pointed his pistol at Martin, roughly at stomach level. "Stop, or it will be the worse for you."

Martin glanced around. There was nobody else in sight; he was alone on a dark, quiet road with a man holding a gun. He pulled at the reins, halted the carts and waited to see what would happen next.

"Strip," the soldier ordered.

"What?" Martin would have stared at the soldier, wondering what he had in mind.

The soldier grabbed hold of Martin's hat and unfastened his neckcloth. Martin did not mention the nine shillings and sixpence he had hidden inside a "parcel of hay" in the crown of his hat. When the soldier waved the pistol at him and told him to give him as much money as he had, Martin removed the fivepence halfpenny in copper from his waistcoat pocket and tossed it angrily into the hat. He watched in some frustration as the soldier clapped the hat on his head and stalked into the night. No doubt shaken, Martin flicked the reins, and his cart jolted into slow motion. He had not gone far before the soldier again loomed out of the dark. There was the ominous click of somebody cocking a well-oiled pistol, and once again the soldier ordered Martin to stop.

"Give me your coat!"

Tearing off his blue greatcoat, Martin threw it into the body of the cart for the soldier to recover. "Wait," he said, "there is a parcel in the pocket; my master's nightcap. May I get it?"

The soldier magnanimously handed it over to him and once more vanished into the dark. This time Martin was allowed to continue in peace. By the time he got home to Janet, his wife, it was nearly one in the morning, but if he was poorer than he had been, at least he was unhurt.

John Maccon was another carter, a young man under 21. He worked for Walter Bold of Dalkeith, who was a dealer in skins as well as running a stable. About half-past six in the morning of the 11th October, Maccon was driving his cart from Dalkeith to Bank house on the Heriot Road when he passed a man in a long greatcoat. The rain was pelting down, so the wheels of his cart splashed through muddy puddles and droplets formed on the brim of Maccon's hat, to drip annoyingly down his face. The weather made him too miserable to talk to the man, who did not speak to him. A mile or two further south, Maccon passed the same great-coated man, standing at the side of the road in the rain. Again, he drove past without speaking.

Another half mile passed and as he negotiated a dip in the road near Crookston Mill Maccon saw the man in the long coat for the third time that morning. This time the man stepped forward, presented a pistol and ordered Maccon to get down off the cart and hand over all his money.

Carters were not among the wealthy elite, so Maccon's five shillings and sixpence would hardly have made the highwayman wealthy.

"And your watch," the highwayman demanded.

Maccon unfastened his watch and handed that over as well. Holding the watch in a surprisingly slender hand, the highwayman seemed satisfied and ordered Maccon to carry on. Maccon did so and bitterly watched the thief coming off the road about another mile to the south. Maccon continued with his journey, stopping at a place called Pencloth to water and feed the horses. While he was there, Maccon naturally told everybody what had happened to him and when the servants had fed the horses, he mounted the fittest and rode on to Bankhouse, a little down the road. When a group of people asked what was to do, Maccon described the highwayman and asked a coachman if he had seen anybody like that.

"I have," the coachman replied.

Encouraged, Maccon rode on to Weatherstone and asked James Mein, the factor, if he had seen the highwayman. Mein said that he had not only seen the man, but he was in the nearby toll house.

In the days before a professional police force, people were more inclined to act themselves, so Maccon recruited a couple of local men from Bankhouse, James Gavinloch and James Hill and together they stormed into the toll house. Recognising the highwayman right away, Maccon pointed him out for his companions to "grip." As one man held the highwayman tight, the others searched him and found a loaded pistol, five shillings and, tied to the waistband of his trousers, Maccon's watch. There could hardly have been more proof of guilt. With three men around him, the highwayman could not resist when they bundled him into a cart and took him to Bankhouse. No doubt growling, he was sat in a corner and carefully watched until Mr Thomson, the local Justice of the Peace first questioned him, discovered his name was John Campbell, and then escorted him to the local constable, William Scott, the weaver, who placed him under arrest.

Scott escorted Campbell all the way to Edinburgh and handed him to Henry Davidson in the sheriff clerk's office. After some intense interrogation, the sheriff officers discovered that the highwayman's real name was Joseph Gibson. According to his own story, he was born in Ireland and joined the 6th Dragoons. When Horse Guards posted the dragoons to Scotland, Gibson came with them, but military life did not agree with him, so he deserted on the 1st October 1812. After lodging with a labourer in Edinburgh's Canongate, he left the house on the 10th and, unsure what to do or where to go next; he walked to a road that led to Musselburgh.

So far, Gibson's story is plausible. He next said that he now met a carter, who must have been James Martin, and asked if he would exchange clothes with him. There would have been some logic in the question, for Gibson still wore the uniform of the 6th Dragoons, which was a bit distinctive for a deserter. What was less believable is that Martin agreed to hand over his clothes, without taking the dragoon's uniform in return. Gibson emphatically denied that he took any of Martin's money. Gibson explained that he removed his uniform jacket and cap and left it at the door of a house.

When Gibson appeared before the High Court in December, the jury listened to his story. Gibson confessed that he had robbed John Maccon but pleaded not guilty to robbing James Martin. The jury tended to believe Martin's account rather than Gibson's and found the Irishman guilty. He was sentenced to be hanged at the west end of Edinburgh's Tolbooth on Wednesday 13th January 1813. Gibson's sordid career as a highwayman lasted two days and ended at the end of a rope.

Trouble on the king's highway

Nineteenth-century Midlothian roads were not always quiet. There were coal carts, tradesmen's carts, butcher's carts, stagecoaches, Royal Mail coaches, pedlars and various types of wanderers as well as men and women walking or riding to work or home. Most of the time, the travellers passed each other with a casual nod and continued with their business, but there were occasions when words were exchanged – or worse.

On the night of the 14th February 1821, Francis Wood and Benjamin Beck were travelling south from Edinburgh, heading towards Moffat. Wood was a carrier, a man who spent his life carting goods from one place to another, while Beck was keeping him company on the section of the road between Edinburgh and Penicuik.

Wood was in front, sitting on the cart and gently walking the horse forward, while Beck was further behind, more sauntering than marching as they covered the ground to Penicuik, the first stop of the journey in those more leisurely days. A full moon highlighted the contours of the Pentland ridge and glossed across the Midlothian plain that stretched on their left, with the friendly house-lights cheerfully pin-pricking through the night. A man was walking toward them, about forty or fifty yards away; Beck lifted a hand in greeting and then turned around at the sound of footsteps. A second hefty-looking man was hurrying up to him from behind.

Without any preamble, the man demanded to know where Beck came from and where he was going. Beck admitted right away that he was a Dumfriesshire man, which seemed to irritate the stranger.

"The people in Dumfriesshire," the man said, "are all dissolute and profane."

Taken slightly aback by this unexpected attack on his home county, Beck said that there "were many respectable people among them," which was quite a mild response. However, that was Beck's last show of patience. In his own words, he was "easily agitated" and so when the man refused to apologise, he grew heated and as he said later "some words then arose". Given that people can be quite defensive of the places from where they come, it was not surprising that he should defend Dumfriesshire from a verbal attack.

As so often happens, high words led to anger and threats. Beck later admitted that he had no clear memory of what happened, or perhaps he chose not to remember, but at one point the stranger spoke about "cudgelling" which meant attacking with a heavy stick.

It was at that point that Wood became involved. He must have been listening to the argument, and when the man began issuing threats, he joined in with a menacing "Will you?" Only two words, but when uttered in such a situation, they can carry a lot of meaning.

Forgetting his part in the proceedings, Beck tried to act the peacemaker, asking the two men not to hit each other. The stranger, who was William Steele, a Penicuik gardener, had too hot a temper for that and Wood was not a man to back down. Steele called Wood "a damned bastard" and promised he would "knock him to eternity." He tried his best to follow up his words as Wood came off his perch in the cart and came for him. Steele waited until he came close then lifted a stout stick and cracked Wood across the side of the head, sending him reeling against the cart and hurting his left ear.

Wood lifted a rack-pin - a sizeable length of rounded timber –from the cart and swung at Steele, knocking off his hat and making him fall back. Steele lay for a moment or two and then rose to his feet.

"If I had you at Penicuik," Steele roared, "I would lay your heels fast!"

"Come back and get your hat," Wood yelled, "and I will give you my stick!"

Steele called his bluff, running at Wood to continue the fight. However, Wood was not bluffing; he swung the rack-pin again, sending Steele to the ground a second time.

When he saw that Wood had felled Steele, Beck moved to help, while Wood moved quickly to his horse, which was inclined to be a bit skittish. With the horse under control, Wood continued with the cart. Steele lay on the ground, bleeding from a wound in the back of his head and moaning. "I'll help," Beck said, and lifted Steele to the side of the road and made him as comfortable as he could. By that time the man Beck had waved to only a few hectic moments before had reached them. He was a local named George Scott, and Beck asked him to look after the injured Steele.

"He gave me a damned sore lug," Wood said, indicating his battered and swollen ear. Blood flowed freely, covering the side of his head and smearing his face and hand. When they arrived at James Dodds' inn at Penicuik, Wood told the story of how he had been attacked and immediately asked for fresh water to wash the blood away. Dodds knew Wood from previous visits and thought him quiet, sober and peaceable.

In the meantime, Scott had tried to rouse Steele and was shocked to see that he appeared stone dead. Calling for help, he carried the body to the house of David Strachan and called for a surgeon. When Dr Renton examined Steele, he found there was nothing he could do. What Renton termed "a severe laceration on the back of the head" had killed him.

The next morning Wood and Beck left the inn, blithely unaware of the death until a sheriff officer hurried after them. He grabbed hold of Beck and immediately charged him with killing Steele. There was a moment's confusion as Beck stared at the officer, and then Wood stepped forward.

"It was I who did the deed," he confessed and gave no resistance as the officer led him back, first to Penicuik and eventually into Edinburgh to face trial for culpable homicide. It was July 1821 before Wood stood at the bar at the High Court, pleaded not guilty and told a story that was slightly different from that of Beck.

He said that Steele had come at them with threatening language, which tied in with Beck's version, but said that he had been on the cart when Steele had attacked him. He also stated that when Steele hit him a second time, he had taken the stick from him and thumped him back. So far, there are no significant differences, just twists of memory. However, Wood's recollection of the next few seconds varied from Beck's. He said that once somebody had hit him, Steele ran away, looked over his shoulder, tripped and fell heavily, landing on his head. It appeared that Wood was saying that the fall killed Steele rather than anything he had done to him.

The jury considered their verdict and seemed to favour Beck's version of events. They found Wood guilty of culpable homicide. Although the judge did not argue their decision, he decided that a short sentence would suffice. As Wood had already spent weeks in jail and had lost his business, which was the sole support for his family, he imposed a sentence of only two months in prison. However, it was an example of the dangers that even a routine journey could have in nineteenth-century Midlothian.

Rude Driving

Road rage and drunken behaviour on the highway are not new occurrences, but the penalties have altered through time. On 27th September 1737, a bunch of young men had been in Edinburgh and were riding back home to Dalhousie, very much the worse for wear having spent considerable time and money in the capital's drinking establishments. The men were David Murray, tenant in Dalhousie, with his servants William Forrest and William Marshall, together with John Macdonald, who was also a servant, but of William Wotherspoon, another Dalhousie tenant.

The men were riding their horses and driving a herd of spare mounts, some laden with meal they had bought in Edinburgh, when they met a coach driving in the opposite direction. Ornate and luxurious, pulled by matching black horses, the coach was obviously the property of a prominent nobleman, who would expect anybody else to give him respect. Half drunk and spread out across the whole width of the road, the men laughed at the sight of the coach and blocked its passage until one of the coachmen, dressed in splendid livery, dismounted to approach them.

"This is my Lord Arniston's coach," the servant said. "I would be obliged if you could allow My Lord's coach so much of the highway that he might pass you by."

Robert Dundas of Arniston was one of the most important men in the area. A prominent lawyer, he was also the sitting Tory MP for Edinburghshire, Solicitor General for Scotland, Lord Advocate and soon to be a judge in the Court of Session, Dundas was not a man to be taken lightly.

Despite all the power and grace of the man in the carriage, Murray and his cronies replied that they would not move, and continued to make the evening raucous with their laughter. The servant tried again, informing Murray that Anne Gordon, her Ladyship was also in the carriage, with other people of quality, and requested again that he should have free passage on the king's highway.

This time, Murray and his friends not only refused passage with what was termed "scurrilous language" but also pushed and struck at both his Lordship's servants and his horses. When a chaise rattled up the road behind Arniston's coach, two of the riders trotted forward and turned it back, before subjecting Arniston and his companions to another volley of oaths, adding some threats for good measure. When one of the sacks of meal tipped off a horse onto the road, they demanded that the Lord Advocate place the sack back on the horse.

Probably recognising that he was powerless against a mob of drunken hooligans, Arniston complied, although doubtless seething inside as he replied to their foul-mouthed taunts with a polite smile. Eventually, Marshall and his boys allowed the Lord Advocate past, and for them, the incident was closed. Arniston thought differently. Either he or his servants recognised the drunks, and Arniston organised the forces of authority to pursue and bring them to justice. As the drunken rioters had not seriously hurt anybody or stolen anything, the law could only drag the culprits to a Justice of the Peace court, which passed the most severe sentence it could. Marshall, Forrest and Macdonald had to spend fourteen days in prison, and then remain behind bars until they found security for their good behaviour for the next three years. That was bad enough, but the judge added public humiliation to the sentence by ordering all three to stand shackled to the pillory in Dalkeith on two separate market days with a placard prominently displayed on their breasts. INSOLENT RIOTER, it read, and one wonders for which crime they were being punished more, rioting or rudeness to the Lord Advocate and his lady wife.

On the 6th October, the three men stood padlocked to the pillory in front of a restless crowd. Word had spread that a gang of Murray's wilder friends planned to rescue them from their plight so that a company of infantry from Major-General Thomas Wetham's 8th Regiment of Foot marched into Dalkeith to keep order and ensure the guilty men endured all their sentence. The moral of this story is: If you are intent on insulting the Lord Advocate on the king's highway, at least wear a mask.

Runaway

Today there are electric cars, hybrid cars and driverless cars, yet in the old days, there was also a variety of traffic, with wagons, post-chaises, farm-carts, stagecoaches and dog-carts. Despite their different sizes and functions, they all had one thing in common; their horses needed careful attention on the road. Or did they? Perhaps the horses knew as well as the drivers where they were going and how to get there. The following anecdote from October 1792 shows the high intelligence of some horses.

When an unnamed gentleman had travelled from Midlothian to Edinburgh to visit a friend, his servants left the carriage unattended as they retrieved him. Seeing their opportunity to escape, the horses bolted, with their master's dog running happily behind. The servants ran after the coach, shouting to no avail as the horses turned three corners in quick succession with the carriage leaning over at an acute angle without falling.

Familiar with the route, the horses took the road to Dalkeith, increasing their speed from a trot to a gallop with no need for a driver until they came to the gibbet toll bar at Newington. When the turnpike-keeper – the man who operated the toll bar - saw the carriage charging toward him, he hastily raised the bar in case there was a nasty accident. However, three coal carts were coming from the Dalkeith side, and the coach came to a halt. The horses waited patiently until the coal carts had passed, leading the turnpike-keeper to believe somebody was driving the coach. When he came out to take his fee, the horses immediately moved off again, dragging the coach behind them and with the dog barking joyously.

The coach rolled on, all the six miles to Dalkeith, where the horses pulled up in a neat turn outside Mrs Johnstone's White Hart Inn and waited there for the stable lads to look after them. Who needs driverless cars when horses can do the job?

Overall, travel on Midlothian's roads could be quite eventful in the days before the internal combustion engine altered everything. Although the speed of modern traffic has probably conveyed highwaymen to history, footpads remain, with the ugly name of muggers and now driverless cars may take the place of driverless horses. Life carries on.

Chapter 14

THE SILVERBURN MURDER

Silverburn is one of these places that does not deserve to have a murder. It is an idyllic hamlet tucked into the flanks of the Pentland Hills a few miles south of Penicuik. Today it is better known for the garden that was on the BBC's programme *The Beechgrove Garden* in 2007, but once it was a working village with a red-roofed blacksmith's forge, a joiner and a collection of cottages. Although the name suggests that miners once worked silver here, that must have been so far ago that it is beyond the memory of man. The only vague recollection of precious metal came from the hopeful dreams of an Irish ditcher who lived in a hut deep in the hills and spent his spare time searching for a pot of gold that he believed to be buried somewhere under the Black Hill. However, in the 1830s, Silverburn was the scene of one of the most poignant murders in all Midlothian, with the victim thought of as one of the gentlest women of the area.

Her name was Catherine Laing, and she was the daughter of Andrew Laing, the Silverburn joiner. Born in 1818, Catherine was the sweetest tempered of all the Laing's children, a girl it was a pleasure to know. When she was a schoolgirl, her sister and one of her brothers were all struck with what was then called "a virulent fever," which eventually hit her as well. Her parents must have been distraught when three of their children sickened and, one by one, began to die. After weeks of suffering and fighting the fever, Catherine survived.

All the time that she lay in her sick-bed, she had never neglected her school work, so when Catherine was sufficiently recovered to return to Sunday school, she was not behind the rest of her class.

Andrew Laing was as generous as he was hard-working, so when he learned that a local youth required a home, he opened his door and offered his hospitality. William Mackay became like a part of the family; he was a brother to Catherine's surviving brother, an apprentice to Andrew and a companion to Catherine. Indeed, he was so much a companion to Catherine that people began to talk, and there were sly winks and many nudgings of sharp elbows into ribs when the pair appeared, walking side-by-side. William was a model youth, a hard worker, a steady church-attender, sober and polite. He was the sort of young man that any parent would wish for a son-in-law but apparently not the kind of man that all girls hoped to marry, and that was the nub of the brewing tragedy. There were a few years between William and Catherine, with William being five years Catherine's senior, but such a small gap was nothing to the path of true love. Unfortunately, only one of the two believed that they were suited.

After seven years of exposure to Catherine's charms, William Mackay was utterly smitten. Even after he left the Laing's home to pursue his career, he followed Catherine everywhere, and when she responded with her customary kindness, he believed that she reciprocated his feelings. So when William asked Catherine to marry him, and she gently turned him down, William was devastated. He had built his life-long hopes on marrying Catherine, and now his future seemed only black. Physically, William slid downhill, and although he still attended church, his speech and ideas were anything but Christian as he openly contemplated suicide. It is possible that he even gave dark mutterings about seeking revenge on Catherine for daring to decline his offer.

It was equally evident that William's injured feelings affected Catherine. She hinted to her mother that he might try and injure her, and every night as the dark eased over the hills, she would close the windows, pull tight the shutters and ensure that they were securely locked. When her mother asked why she did so, she replied that she was scared in case William came into the house at night.

Even as she took these precautions, Catherine worried about the health of the man she had rejected. Taking her mother aside, she asked her privately if it would not be best if she married William, rather than have him hurt so much. Her mother asked if she would be happy with him, and she answered: "no. I could never love him, but nor do I wish him to suffer."

"Then do not marry him," Catherine's mother advised.

At ten in the evening of the first of December 1837, Catherine sat quietly at home sewing diligently as the open fire kept her warm, despite the Pentland wind that rattled at the window at her side. It was a beautiful scene that could have graced any picture-book: The rural background with shapely hills, the neat, red-tiled cottages in the hamlet and the young girl quiet beside the fire. The sudden report of the gun was deafening and was followed immediately by the clatter of shattering glass and Catherine's startled yell. The musket ball hit Catherine in the arm, passed through and into her body, tearing both lungs. Catherine fell at once, vomiting blood as her parents rushed to try and help her. Cleaning Catherine up, they held her close as she choked, spitting blood onto the front of her dress as her sewing lay unheeded on the floor. Her father carried her upstairs, and her mother bundled her up to bed and listened as she asked to speak to the local minister, the Reverent Moncrieff.

In great pain and coughing up blood, Catherine told the minister that she thought William was her murderer, "he has threatened me before," she said.

With no policeman to call on, the locals took things in hand themselves. Organising into small groups, they searched the area, probing into the night-time hills, where a cold winter wind sliced through the brown heather. The searchers knocked on doors, checked outbuildings and barns and even entered the policies of nearby Penicuik House. They were not successful: William Mackay had vanished into the dark.

There is some doubt about the subsequent movements of Mackay. It is known that he ran into the grounds of Penicuik House to hide, and people supposed that he spent most of the night up a tree near the large pond, but his movements at about one in the morning are a bit of a mystery. While one account says that he banged on the gardener's door and asked for paper and pen, another says that is simply not true. If that did happen, the gardener must have been more than a little apprehensive about having a supposed murderer at his door, if indeed the news had yet spread to him. In the meantime, Catherine, after twelve hours of agony, had slipped into a period of peace. Typical of her angelic nature, she asked her parents to forgive her murderer, and moments later she died. About two hours after that, the procurator fiscal and the sheriff appeared to take charge of matters.

Around two in the afternoon, William appeared again, carrying a long fowling-piece and a pistol. This time there is no dispute about his movements. He met one of the gardeners and asked for news of Catherine.

"She's dead," the gardener told him curtly, no doubt eyeing the weapons and wondering if he was to be next.

"Well," William said, "having taken one life I must also take my own." He ran away, and a few minutes later, the gardener heard the loud crack of a gunshot. William had placed the muzzle of his musket in his mouth and pulled the trigger. The heavy lead shot shattered his skull to pieces. When his body was found, the paper and pen were in his pocket: the last letter to Catherine and his will: He had no intention of living. As the winter daylight faded, sombre men carried William's body to his parent's house. Catherine was buried the following Monday in the churchyard at Penicuik, with a vast crowd to say goodbye.

It was a tragedy typical of the nineteenth century when men and women lived by their emotions and passions ran high.

Chapter 15

THE LAST HANGING

In an age where respectability meant everything, George Dickson was a highly respectable man. He farmed at Cousland, a few miles from Dalkeith, was reputedly the oldest yeoman in Scotland and kept regular hours and habits. People knew him by name and reputation as a steady, reliable man, and he would have looked for no higher honour.

On 30th f November 1826, George Dickson attended Dalkeith Market, as he had done scores of times before. Markets were vital to the farmers; they were the buckle that fastened the farming community together and the place where farmers met to discuss prices, livestock and labour. Markets were gatherings where farmers compared the success of their techniques with those of their neighbours and rivals. Farmers attended markets to make money, sell the beasts that were no longer productive or buy those they hoped would improve their own breeding stock. To the outsider, the talk of stots and stirks, tups and gimmers, threshers and balers would be as incomprehensible as Latin and as far removed from their day-to-day life, but for the farmers from the fertile Lothian fields, the market was a second home. In the fast-changing years of the nineteenth century where innovation was king and only the steady turn of the seasons was constant, the market provided sanity and conversation.

Dalkeith's Corn Exchange was the largest and most important grain market in Scotland, so, on market days the roads were crammed with incoming farmers on horseback, dealers in gigs and gentlemen in four-in-hands, while the lowly labourers would rely on foot-leather and the power of their legs to get them there. The streets were filled with carts and horses while steady-eyed men in broadcloth exchanged quiet greetings, said little and noticed all.

Markets were also where men often drank a little more than was good for them and left with the whisky humming in their heads and crisp bank notes or gold coins a welcome weight in their pockets. But if the farmers knew the value of markets to the local economy, so did the criminals.

When George Dickson left the market at about five that November evening, the sky was already dark, and a slight wind was rustling the stark branches of the leaf-stripped trees. He would huddle into his greatcoat, pull his broad hat closer onto his head and guide his horse onto the road for Cousland. Unlike many others at the market, Dickson had not lingered at any of the inviting hostelries of Dalkeith, but as soon as his business was complete, he visited his father-in-law, a merchant by the name of Alexander Wilson. They passed a few pleasant minutes, and then Dickson mounted his horse and took the straight road by the Cow Bridge and Langside Brae. Respectable, hard-working men such as Dickson did not waste time or money in a market-day public house.

Once he was outside Dalkeith, there were some lonely stretches on the road, but Dickson was a local man and knew his way. As he was passing the foot of Langside Brae, where a dense plantation on the left made the gloomy winter night even darker, he looked around, negotiated the horse around a slight overflow from the burn and listened to the hiss of wind through the trees. Dickson checked his silver hunter watch: Ten past five. He was making good time and should be home within half an hour. There were some piles of stones waiting to be broken up for road-repairs beside the road: Dickson spared them only a casual glance but started when a shadowy figure emerged at his side.

Dickson did not have time to react as the man grabbed hold of the reins of his horse. He looked downward, sure he recognised him by his saturnine, hard-featured face but not entirely sure where he had seen him before. The slender curve of the two-day-old moon did not give him much light for recognition. Dickson did know that the man held a large stick, a cudgel nearly, freshly cut and with a viciously-heavy knot at the business end. Before Dickson had time to react, the man swung the cudgel at him, catching him a smart crack on the head. Dickson did the only thing he could to try and escape; he kicked his heels into the flank of his horse, so it reared up and landed with a thump just in front of his attacker.

"If I had been wearing spurs," Dickson later said, grimly, "there would be no need for a trial."

As the attacker's grip on Dickson's reins loosened, another man appeared on the opposite side and seized hold of him. Dickson again kicked in his heels, trying to break free of both men and hoping that the flailing hooves of his horse would do some damage to one or both of them. Or rather some of them, for Dickson became aware of another two men surrounding him. The first man swung his stick again, catching Dickson such a mighty blow on the head that he fell off his horse, to lie stunned on the ground. He felt the stick land again, felt the warm blood flow onto his face and knew that somebody was picking his pockets but was temporarily unable to do anything about it.

As the second man also put his hands in his pockets, Dickson realised where he had seen them before. It had only been a few days since they came to him at Cousland, asking for a job. He had nothing for them to do so turned them away: Was this their way of seeking revenge? He looked around; one of the men was wearing a red waistcoat with sleeves the colour of dirty stone. The others wore dark clothes. One was much younger than the others and had taken no part in the attack. After that, Dickson stopped thinking about his attackers and more about how to save himself as he thought the man in the red waistcoat said:

"Murder the bugger: murder him!"

Dickson flinched at another blow to his head, and then all four attackers scurried away into the dark fastness of the plantation. Dickson heard them moving for a few moments and then they were gone. Pulling himself upright, he fingered his injuries; there was blood flowing from cuts to his head and some bruising to his chest, but he would live. He checked his pockets: his attackers had stolen his silver hunter watch, a letter from his wife and a copy of the *Scotsman* newspaper. Slowly mounting his horse, Dickson headed back to Dalkeith. The whole affair had only taken a few moments.

At Cleugh Bridge Dickson met John Smith, a ploughman, and told him what had happened. He also asked Smith to follow the men who had attacked him.

Back with his father-in-law by a quarter to six, the shaken and bloodied Dickson sent for Dr Scott, who dressed his wounds and thought he was "seriously injured." It may have been Scott who ordered a chaise to take him home. The next day Dickson returned to Dalkeith and told his tale to James Turnbull, the sheriff officer. Turnbull asked if he could name his attackers, which he could not, but he did give a detailed description. Turnbull said he thought he knew the men involved. Picking up four men he thought may be involved, Turnbull brought them to the sheriff office, where he asked Dickson if they were the right culprits. When Dickson said that they were, two of the men protested that they had been elsewhere at the time, but that did not shake Dickson's conviction.

The first man was William Thomson, whom Dickson thought was the hard-faced man who had grabbed his reins and attacked him with the cudgel. He was a labourer from Newbigging near Inveresk. The second man was James Thomson, his brother, and the third was John Fram, their cousin, also from Newbigging. Fram wore a red waistcoat with greyish sleeves which was shockingly familiar. The fourth was a youth named William Leslie, the youngster who had taken no part in the actual attack. Turnbull had the three adults safely put away in Edinburgh's Calton Jail while Leslie was questioned to see what he knew.

William Leslie was a 15-year-old labourer, a neighbour of the Thomson's in Newbigging. He said that William Thomson employed him on a casual basis breaking stones at two shillings and sixpence [12.5 pence] a week, and on the day of the market, William Thomson asked him to go to Dalkeith to find work with a Mr Forbes. They left Newbigging at about three in the afternoon, with James Fram and James Thomson accompanying them. The Thomsons both wore blue coats and fustian trousers, dark clothes that merged with the rapidly darkening day. About half a mile outside Dalkeith, the Thomsons, left the highway for a plantation beside a small bridge, where they cut hefty lengths of wood. When Leslie asked why, William Thomson told him they were making "hammer shafts." By then, the winter daylight was fading, and Leslie wished he had not come. He waited on the road until the Thomsons and Fram emerged with their lengths of new-cut wood. When Leslie asked why they did not go into Dalkeith to see Mr Forbes, William Thomson told him that Forbes "would not be at home." As time passed, home was where Leslie wished he were. Instead, Leslie waited by the plantation as the Thomsons, and Fram paced up and down the road. He did not know what they planned next, if indeed they had any plan at all.

Just after five in the evening, they heard the slow drumming of hooves as a horseman trotted from the direction of Dalkeith. Leslie remained beside the dense trees of the plantation as William Thomson slipped down to the nearest pile of stones. In the gathering dark, he did not recognise the rider, but he could plainly see William Thomson emerge from the rocks to grab hold of his reins. Leslie watched as William Thomson swung his stick, cracking the rider across the side of the head. He saw James Thomson run forward next, grabbed hold of the horse's head and thumped the rider across the chest with his stick. Only then did Fram appear, but either he was outside Leslie's line of vision, or he was a mere bystander, for Leslie thought he was not otherwise involved in the attack. Leslie was confident that neither Fram nor anybody else suggested murdering Dickson.

Instead, what Leslie did hear was Dickson shouting: "stop, stop, and I'll give you what I have," which is not quite as Dickson remembered things. He saw the Thomsons haul Dickson off his horse and pick his pocket and then everybody ran away. Although Dickson was sure they vanished inside the plantation, Leslie said they ran toward Newbigging, until William suggested going to his sister-in-law's house. James looked at the documents they had stolen, decided they were not worth having and immediately threw them over a bridge. The sticks followed soon after.

Leslie was the youngest there, but also the slowest as all the others left him trailing behind as they fled. Much later he found them in Janet Thomson's house in Inveresk. Janet was Thomson's sister and shared her home with James and Fram. They all stayed the night. Next morning William showed the booty: Dickson's silver watch. At that time Leslie still did not know who the victim had been although he knew Dickson well enough to recognise him in daylight. That fact makes Dickson's immediate recognition of his attackers slightly suspect, given the speed of events and the darkness of the night.

While Leslie was giving his account of the robbery, a farm worker named Robert Somerville found the discarded letters. He brought them to Wilson, who passed them on to the authorities. Shortly afterwards, David Cumming, a ploughman at Smeaton, had seen his horse's feet kick up a *Scotsman* newspaper; he handed that over as well.

In January 1827, when the case appeared before the High Court, both Thomsons and Fram pleaded not guilty. They gave alibis, with William Thomson claiming to have been at his mother-in-law's house in Dalkeith, while James Thomson and John Fram claimed they were both at home in Newbigging. Leslie's testimony suggested that they were not telling the truth, and then a succession of witnesses said they had seen the accused men going toward Dalkeith at the time they claimed they were elsewhere.

There was an Inveresk boy named John Collins who saw the foursome on the road, as well as a Cowpits collier named William Naismith, while a man named Peter Borthwick from Whitecraig Cottage, saw the accused around four o'clock. Borthwick saw them again at the back of six near Inveresk Brae, walking in the direction of Newbigging, as did John Smith, a Langside ploughman. Ann Ross and Christian

Thomson were confident they saw all four men around four o'clock. Of them all, John Smith's evidence was perhaps the more damning as he saw them walking in both directions; he saw William Thomson carrying a stick and heard what he described as a "noise like a horse leaping." When Smith met Dickson, he said he was "confused and bleeding."

The final witness was Alexander Merilees, another neighbour from Newbigging. Sometime between nine and ten on the morning of the market day, Thomson approached him in the street and asked him to come into Dalkeith to "rumble a cove." The phrase is cant, the speech used by the criminal underclass, and means to attack a man. When the Lord Justice Clerk heard it, he blamed the crime on the influence of a book called *The Life of David Haggart* which had been published in 1821 and purported to be the life story of a criminal condemned to hang in Edinburgh. "One of the most infamous works ever printed," the Lord Justice Clerk said: a statement that may well have boosted sales.

Rather than accompany Thomson on his rumbling visit, Merilees walked in the opposite direction, to Prestonpans. Much later, when he judged it safe, he returned to Newbigging, but by then William Thomson was long gone. Probably relieved, Merilees wandered into Ferguson's ale-house in Inveresk instead. Sometime after six Fram burst in, "much heated" as Merilees put it. He saw Merilees at once, asked him to wait and quickly dashed away. Well, it was no hardship for Merilees to linger in an ale-house, but Fram did not come back. Merilees remained for a few hours and staggered home, entirely unaware his innocent actions would help prove William Thomson's character as an evil man.

When the Lord Advocate heard all the facts of the case, he said it was "one of the most atrocious cases of robbery ever brought before a court or presented to a jury." He had no hesitation in asking for a guilty verdict and added that it "called for capital punishment." His words informed the jury that they had the responsibility of possibly ending the lives of the accused, so they hedged a little by finding all three guilty but recommending mercy for James Thomson and Fram. Both these men, the jury claimed, had been dominated by William Thomson who the newspapers described as "a man of forbidding appearance." In contrast, James had only a "wild aspect."

The judge accepted the guilty verdict but not the merciful codicil; he sentenced all three to death. The hangings were to take place on Thursday the 1st of March 1827, "at or near Dalkeith." As it transpired, merciful authority reprieved the death penalty for two of the men, while William Thomson was hanged on Thursday the 1st of March.

As executions were infrequent in Dalkeith – Thomson's big day was the first in living memory and the last that was ever to take place in the town – the event generated much interest. If we are to believe the reports, the good people of Dalkeith tended to regard the hanging as a blight on their town and either closed their doors and windows and refused to watch or left the area for the day. However, the people from the country districts had no such scruples and assembled outside the tolbooth from early morning to watch this free entertainment, or perhaps to offer final support for a man that some of them would know well.

William Thomson had been held in Calton Jail in Edinburgh, frequently visited by his wife. On the night before the execution, she saw him for the last time; a bittersweet meeting that both knew marked a full stop in both their lives. Shortly after half past nine in the morning, a curious crowd began to gather, growing ever larger as the time came for Thomson to leave on his last journey. By half-past, twelve thousand were waiting around the jail. Inside, the ministers and wardens took a glass of port with Thomson, shook his hand and escorted him into one of the three carriages that drew up at the entrance to the jail.

If people hoped for drama, they were disappointed. Thomson seemed calm and even relaxed. The prison chaplain and other officials were sombre compared to the slightly smiling footpad. The carriages grumbled on, past the gawping crowds and south toward Thomson's destiny. They arrived in Dalkeith shortly after two in the afternoon and pushed through the gathering to disembark at the tolbooth opposite the ancient church of St Nicholas.

Busy workmen had already erected the scaffold in the street in front of the tolbooth, and perhaps Thomson glanced at the gallows noose swinging, silent and sinister, above the trapdoor as he was ushered inside for a psalm and final prayers. After that interlude, his time was short. He was escorted outside, to mount the steps to the platform as the crowd removed their hats as a final mark of respect. He had a last prayer; he would look at the mass of faces, perhaps recognising friends and relations, perhaps bitter about life; maybe regretting how his actions would affect his wife and six-year-old son.

Then he stepped onto the trap door, and the executioner pulled the white hood over his head; Thomson gave the signal. The trap sprung open, and Thomson dropped; the noose tightened, and he died. The crowd would watch for a while and slowly dissipate; if his wife was there, she might have been the last to leave.

It is hard to imagine an execution in Dalkeith now. The tolbooth still exists, recently renovated in the town's conservation area. If the visitor looks at the ground outside, he or she may see a group of differently coloured granite setts; they mark where Thomson was hanged; a brief and sombre reminder of a failed criminal and a sordid little crime.

Chapter 16

WHO WERE THE DUELLISTS?

A duel was a matter of honour, usually fought between gentlemen at the point of a sword or the muzzle of a pistol. The idea of duelling to settle a dispute stretches back at least to the middle ages when knights in armour would battle things out with sword and shield. The rules were not formalised until the fourteenth century when the French created the *pas d'armes* where one man, or a group of men desperate to prove their manhood or just plain keen to fight, would challenge all comers to pass a specific spot or be disgraced. This piece of mediaeval madness arose with the rise of romantic chivalry and the notion of gentlemanly honour.

As the popularity of the duel rose, various popes and others with religious or monarchical authority, sought to ban the practice, mainly because thousands of young men were slaughtering each other in the name of honour. In the reign of Henry IV of France, 1589-1610, some four thousand of France's finest died at the point of an opponent's sword, and that was decades before the Three Musketeers began their career of honourable slaughter. France had a formal code of duelling, as had Ireland in 1777. In Scotland, the practice was not as widespread as it was on the continent, although gentlemen carried swords and were quite likely to use them on very slight provocation.

Duels could be over quickly with an exchange of fire and nobody hurt, or a brief clash of blades and a flesh wound settling the argument.

They could also be nasty, with one man killed and the other fleeing from the prospect of the gallows. Even a wound could easily be fatal, with pistols firing a heavy lead ball that could smash bones or cause terrible damage to internal organs. In the days when guns were notorious for their inaccuracy, it was sensible to aim at the broadest part of the body, which meant the area between the hips. Many wounds were in the groin, and if the argument was over a woman, rather than a point of honour, some duellists seemed to take particular satisfaction in aiming at this very vulnerable area.

There were some significant duels in Scotland, including one in 1731, when George Lockhart of Lee, writer and active Jacobite, was killed. Another, in 1787, saw Sir John MacPherson, a Skye man and former Governor-General of India, exchange fire with Major Browne who had held the position of British Resident at the court of Shah Alam II, the sixteenth Mughal Emperor. Despite the participants' high positions and presumably military background, neither man was hurt. Arguably the best-known Scottish duel was fought at Cardenden in Fife in 1826; this encounter has been called the last fatal duel in Scotland as the linen merchant David Landale duelled with George Morgan, his bank manager. Now that would draw crowds today! Landale killed Morgan and was found not guilty of murder. He was fortunate, for when Major Campbell of the 21st Foot, the Royal Scots Fusiliers defeated Captain Boyd of the same regiment in a duel in 1808, a judge believed it was murder and ordered him executed.

Much less frequent were so-called "petticoat duels" between women. Probably the best known in Britain was fought in London, in 1792, when Mrs Elphinstone called on Lady Ameria Braddock and complimented her on retaining her looks. Unfortunately, she added that she must have been a real beauty forty years ago, at which Lady Ameria claimed she was not yet thirty. When Mrs Elphinstone said she was sixty-one, Her Ladyship challenged her to a duel, and they met with pistols and swords. The contest ended with a nick on Mrs Elphinstone's arm, but the fact the women fought at all must have spread speculation on Lady Ameria's real age to a much wider audience.

Although Midlothian was hardly a hot-spot for duelling, there were some occasions when men faced each other along the length of a long-barrelled pistol, or at the business end of a sword. Unfortunately for the historian, if fortunately for the participants, the full name of the duellists was seldom recorded. However, what we do know about what was arguably the last genuine duel in Scotland is undoubtedly intriguing.

On Thursday 18th February 1841, five men left an inn in Penicuik and travelled a few miles south to the Walstone Muir. History knows two of them by their initials alone: Mr L. and Dr H. These two men were to be the principals in a duel, with two of the others acting as their seconds and the fifth man a surgeon to tend any injured. They had arranged to meet in a quiet spot, known as a "field of honour" where nobody in authority could disturb them. It had been the seconds' task to find this suitably secluded field, if possible on disputed land, to avoid any claims about trespass. The timing was important as well: Duellists often favoured dawn, partly because the light would be sufficiently faint to help hide the participants, and partly because it could give a full night's contemplation after what might have been a drunken challenge. Men sober at dawn may not have the same desire to murder a colleague that they had when in their cups – or the same courage to face the prospect of a yard of sharp steel through their innards.

In this instance, the seconds had not been quite smart enough, for a hint of their intended purpose had leaked out at the inn. Two men followed them out of Penicuik and on to the moor; the duellists looked behind them at the shadowy figures on horseback and wondered if they should continue. They were both quite prepared to risk their lives in an honourable duel, but neither cared to end their existence dangling at the end of a rope: There was neither honour nor dignity in that.

Accordingly, the duelling party returned to the inn in Penicuik, then slipped away again, split up and travelled separately to a new duelling site, so making it very difficult for the two men to follow them all. When they reached the designated location, they discussed how they should proceed. There were various types of duel, and they could not decide which was best, with Dr H. favouring the French system while Mr L. wanted the more straightforward British method. Eventually, they resorted to the traditional system of tossing a coin, with the winner deciding how the participants should kill each other. Somebody tossed the coin, Dr H's second called for heads and nodded as Queen Victoria's profile stared up at them from the grass.

With that detail disposed of, the seconds and the surgeon withdrew hastily to the right, putting considerable distance between themselves and the participants. Dr H and Mr L stood back to back, each holding a long-nosed pistol. It was the first time either had been in such a situation so they would be nervous, possibly trembling as they heard the signal to begin. They paced forward, counting each step, "one, two, three," with Dr H the faster walker, "four, five, six," or perhaps the more keen to get the affair over with, "seven eight, nine." He was first to reach the required number of steps "ten," and fired even as he turned, but either he was too anxious or a very poor shot, for the ball was well wide, passing between the two no-doubt startled seconds.

Mr L. was more composed, turned, aimed and fired seconds later, with the ball speeding in the right direction but missing Dr H as it whizzed past his hand. According to the rules of duelling, that exchange of fire could have ended the affair with honour satisfied, but the challenger had the right to a second chance. So the entire rigmarole was gone through again. It must have been harder to hit with a pistol than it appears in Hollywood films, as both duellists missed again, so Dr H decided to end the nonsense by writing a note that agreed Mr L had made some now-forgotten anatomical discovery related to "physiological phenomenon."

After that one brief venture into the limelight, both duellists withdrew into obscurity so dense that history did not even record their names.

Other duels in the area are worth mentioning, if only briefly, because few details were recorded. One such event occurred in late December 1724, although the exact location is not known, it could be anywhere southward from Edinburgh. The names, likewise, were not written down, although one of the participants was C. U. and may have been Charles Urquhart, attached to, or an officer of, the "Royal Regiment of Scots Fuzileers." The dispute was about nationality as an officer of an English regiment called the Fuzileers (now spelled Fusiliers) "Scots scoundrels, pickpockets, villains" and added that the whole of Scotland was "such like." Not surprisingly, C. U. took offence and challenged the Englishman to a duel. They used swords rather than pistols, and wherever they met, the Scottish officer was the victor, severely wounding the Englishman. Hopefully he learned never to insult Scotland again.

Half a century later, on the First of April 1776, two medical students from Edinburgh University travelled south of the city to Dalkeith to settle their differences. These gentlemen chose pistols rather than swords, paced the obligatory distance, turned and fired. Both missed, with the balls flying nowhere. At that point they could have ended the dispute, with honour satisfied and both having proved their courage. However, they must have been either eager to hurt one another or extremely angry for they insisted on a second shot. Reloading, they again stood back to back, paced the fifteen steps, turned and fired. This time, one man hit the other in the thigh, and that ended the matter.

There may well have been other duels in Midlothian, for the very nature of the beast ensured its secrecy. However, many there were, the dramatic few moments where two men faced each other knowing one could soon be dead or severely injured, must have been a memory that lasted forever.

Chapter 17

THE POACHERS

Throughout the nineteenth century, there was a constant war as the landowners in Midlothian strove to keep poachers from their lands. It was not a war of massive armies or major battles, but one where overworked gamekeepers and their assistants watched over vast swathes of territory by night and day, alone or in small groups. They were defending fertile land from potentially large numbers of enemies, for to judge by the police courts, most weeks there were numbers of men out in the fields with traps or guns, hunting for rabbits or whatever else they could find to supplement their diet.

Poaching was a lottery, for a successful foray depended on many factors, such as whether the gamekeeper was patrolling the area in which the poacher worked, or whether there were pheasants or other types of game present. Even if the keepers caught them, the penalties varied immensely. For example, when a slater named James Miller was caught poaching in the grounds of Penicuik House in September 1859, Sheriff Arkley awarded him 30 days hard labour and ordered to find £10 surety for his good behaviour or face a further six months inside. That same month, Sheriff Hallard only fined two miners, William Denison and Thomas Penicuik, £1 with an alternative of ten days for poaching and assaulting James Brown, who worked for the landowner Ainslie of Costerton. When Brown followed them on the lands he protected, they pulled what was termed "disjointed guns" from their pockets and threatened to "blow his brains into the air" unless he turned back. Justice could be a lottery in the nineteenth century.

Midlothian is a rich land with several significant landowners. The Duke of Buccleuch, the Earl of Roseberry, Ramsay of Whitehill, Dundas of Arniston and the Earl of Dalhousie; the names resounded in the political and social annals of Scotland's elite, but all were firm in keeping people of lower social class from their game.

Most poaching was likely unrecorded as the poachers managed to avoid detection, and even if the keepers caught them, the majority of potential poachers accepted their fate without too much resistance. Others were truculent; when they resisted, the gamekeepers had to fight for their lives.

When times were hard, jobs were few and money short, crime against property, such as theft, increased. The 1840s was one of the worst decades of the century, with bad weather, crop failure, famine in the Highlands and Ireland and political and social turmoil. Not surprisingly, it was also a decade that saw a great deal of poaching. By that time, some of the anti-poaching laws were draconian. For example, if the keepers caught three or more armed men who intended poaching, the culprits were liable to harsh sentences; on the lower end of the scale was three years in prison with hard labour, while the maximum was fourteen years transportation. When the sheriff or judge who handed out the sentences were from the same social circle as the landowner, men caught poaching would know they faced difficult times.

On the 18th of October 1847, a well-known family of poachers named Vickers sallied forth en-masse to try the fertile lands of the Earl of Roseberry around Carrington. There was Alexander, George, Ramsay and William Vickers and a neighbour named William Beveridge. Arming themselves, and, braving a night of biting winds that thrashed the branches of the trees and dragged ragged clouds across the sky, they marched out to try their luck.

The poachers chose the Earl of Roseberry's Aitkendean wood, about half a mile from Carrington, and were threading through the dark undergrowth when they realised they were not alone; there were keepers on the watch. In a situation where armed poachers came into direct contact with armed gamekeepers, there must have been apprehension in both camps. The poachers would know that capture could lead to a lengthy spell in jail and that the law fully supported the keepers, while the gamekeepers would understand that the poachers could be desperate men who could resort to violence to escape capture.

On this occasion, neither side held back. Facing the poachers were four gamekeepers: Archibald White, assistant keeper to Dundas of Arniston, Robert Hume, keeper to the Earl of Dalhousie, John Falconer, assistant keeper to Ramsay of Whitehill and William Liddel, keeper to the Earl of Roseberry. Both groups prepared for confrontation.

The poachers were first to react; Alexander Vickers raised his shotgun and fired. It was a rushed snap-shot through trees in the dark of the night, so most of the pellets flew wide. However, a number struck painfully on the thighs and buttocks of Robert Hume. Naturally, he roared with the sudden pain, and that may have been the stimulus for the other keepers to charge and close with the poachers. The Vickers clan were not men to back down and surged forward to meet the attack. As the keepers punched George Vickers to the ground, William Vickers knocked down Archibald White. After a flurry of blows, both sides withdrew into the darkness, bearing their casualties with them.

Although the poachers arguably got the better of the skirmish, the gamekeepers had the last laugh as they recognised the men they had fought. Alerting the police, the keepers had the poachers arrested. At their trial, the poachers pleaded guilty, putting forward the defence that they were angry and only reacting to their brother's injury. As they had fired first, the jury found them guilty. Alexander and William Vickers were transported for seven years while the judge imprisoned the others for eighteen months.

Sometimes, however, poaching expeditions could have an even more tragic outcome. Poaching was more prevalent in winter than summer, when the nights were long and dark, and clandestine activity was easier. The gamekeepers were well aware of that fact, of course, and kept alert. On the night of the 15th of December 1884, John Fortune, gamekeeper at Roseberry Estate south of Gorebridge, was on his routine patrol, along with twenty-five-year-old John McDiarmid and James Grosset. Grosset had worked in the estate for twenty-nine years; he knew every thicket and field, while McDiarmid was a newcomer to the area, a rabbit trapper who had lived on Roseberry's land a couple of weeks previously. Despite the possibility of meeting poachers, the keepers only carried walking sticks. They were not expecting anything out of the ordinary as they walked beneath a fitful moon, with occasional patches of frost crisping the grass.

It was about half-past two on Saturday morning when the gamekeepers decided to call it a night. It was cold and dark, with only the sound of wind in the trees and the occasional call of a hunting owl to disturb the silence. Grosset returned to his home at Roseberry farm steading, with McDiarmid living not far away. Fortune had a three-mile hike to his house, which was nothing to a man who spent his working life out of doors.

They had not gone far when Grosset heard the distinctive bang of a shotgun and bellowed for Fortune. Sending his wife to rouse McDiarmid, Grosset raced toward the source of the shot, with Fortune and McDiarmid joining a few moments later. Their studded boots echoed as they crossed the bridge at the overflow of the Edgelaw Reservoir and walked quickly toward Westerpark of Redside farm when they heard a shotgun crack again.

Knowing the ground well, Grosset and Fortune did not hesitate, with McDiarmid, younger and keen to prove his worth, a few steps behind. They followed a field edge, climbing up a slope with a fence to mark the boundary, and stopped as they saw two men, undoubtedly poachers, higher up the slope. Both poachers carried shotguns and moved confidently as if aware they were in no danger of arrest. The keepers sunk to their stomachs and watched as the two poachers walked toward them.

Fortune waited until the poachers were around fifteen yards away and suddenly stood up, with the other keepers following his lead.

The poachers would have been shocked to have three gamekeepers abruptly rise from the ground in front of them. They began a slow withdrawal, still holding their shotguns and as dangerous as any cornered wild beast. They must have considered turning and running to hide in the dark, but then a treacherous gust of wind scuffed the clouds from the moon. Grosset, a local man, immediately thought he recognised the poachers. Perhaps he would have been better to say nothing, allow them to escape and pick them up later. Instead, he announced one of their names.

"There is no use running or going on like that," he said. "I know you, Innes."

Grosset saw them as thirty-seven-year-old William Innes and thirty-six-year-old Robert Flockhart Vickers.

As the gamekeepers slowly advanced, the poachers shouted a warning:

"Stand back!"

There would be considerable tension with the two poachers apprehensive about jail, and the keepers face to face with a brace of armed men in a lonely field.

"You take that one," Innes said, the words quite clear to Grosset, "and I'll go for this bugger."

The keepers must have flinched as both poachers lifted their shotguns; Vickers fired first, with his pellets smashing into young McDiarmid's arm and knocked him to the ground. As Grosset bent to see how severely McDiarmid was injured, Innes fired, the shot echoing through the night. Four pellets slammed into Grosset's back and shoulder. He staggered, and Vickers fired the second barrel. The shot smashed into Fortune, hitting him in the lower abdomen.

He fell, immediately aware the wound was severe. "I am shot through the heart," he said, "what will my poor wife do?"

With his two companions down and wounded himself, Grosset moved to check on Fortune, hearing the murmur of voices in the dark.

"Don't let him get off," one of the poachers said. "Load quick and shoot him."

Fortune lay on the ground, feeling his life slip away. "I would have got the little black rascal if the other had not done for me," he whispered to Grosset.

The poachers continued their attack. According to Grosset, Innes lifted his gun again and tried to fire, but with no result as the percussion cap failed.

Grosset told Fortune to lie still and keep quiet as he ran for help. In the moonlit gloom of the night, he saw the poachers reload, with their words sinister, their intent to finish what they had started.

"Load quick," Innes said. "Don't let the bugger get away. Give him another shot."

Leaving his badly wounded companions on the ground, Grosset retreated. He had been the hunter; now he was the hunted, an injured man, in pain and no doubt fearful, with two desperate predators searching for him. He heard the drift of conversation; he heard one of the poachers mentioning that they would get him at the bridge. But Grosset knew the ground well and altered direction toward Edgelaw Farm instead.

Although Edgelaw was in darkness, the shots had wakened Robert Simpson, the farmer. He was eager to help and first brought Grosset into the house and then ordered William Brydon, the grieve, to find the wounded keepers. Brydon wakened one of the farm hands and told him what was happening. With Grosset's directions to guide them, they wheeled a cart from the yard and hurried to find the casualties, fully aware there were dangerous men out there. In the meantime, Simpson ran to Gorebridge to fetch a doctor.

Out on the hill, the poachers looked over the field of battle. One was heard to say: "the buggers are dead enough," and then they hurried after Grosset, but too late to catch him.

The men from Edgelaw farm found that the wounded keepers had tried to crawl toward help. Fortune had managed a couple of hundred yards and collapsed. The farm workers saw the extent of his injuries and decided he was too badly hurt to survive the jolting of a cart so instead carried him home as gently as they could. Fortune seemed slightly delirious, talking to his rescuers as if to the poachers: "You know me," he said, "we've had a dram together, and you won't shoot me." They left him with his wife. 'It was not Innes who shot me," he told her.

As McDiarmid seemed less badly hurt, the Edgelaw men bundled him into a cart for the jolting trip.

When Dr Spalding from Gorebridge arrived at Fortune's house, he made a quick examination and found that the gamekeeper not as severely wounded as he appeared. Many of the lead pellets had embedded into Fortune's silver watch, completely ruining the German silver case cover. The watch had undoubtedly saved his life for the time being, although there were still more than fifty lead pellets lodged in his side. Unfortunately, after a gallant struggle for his life, on the 18th of December 1884, Fortune died of peritonitis. Young McDiarmid, the rabbit catcher, fought for weeks. He had thirty-eight lead pellets in his right arm and for a while, looked as if he would recover. And then, when a concerned nurse was changing his dressing, McDiarmid began to bleed heavily. He finally passed away from loss of blood on the 8th of January 1885. Before he died, he named Robert Vickers as one of the poachers.

Well before McDiarmid died, the county police had been active. Sergeant Adamson was already aware of Vickers and Innes's poaching activities. It was not long since he arrested Innes's brother in Loanhead, so when he knocked on William Innes's door, he was not too surprised to see his suspect lying in bed with a gunshot wound on his jaw. Leaving Innes in bed, Adamson found his shotgun and handed it to a gamekeeper and gun expert named David Brotherstone, who decided that somebody had recently fired it. There was also fresh mud on the gun as if Innes had been out in the fields. Arresting Innes, Adamson took him to Edinburgh Infirmary, placed him under guard and searched for Vickers, whom he stopped shortly afterwards in the open street.

When Innes was well enough to travel, the wardens of Calton jail took him to Rosebery House, where the keepers positively identified him as one of the poachers.

Despite the gamekeepers' certainty in identifying their attackers, the two suspected poachers denied their involvement. The police made their enquiries and unearthed a surprising number of witnesses who claimed to have seen both suspects in various places the night of the battle. The witnesses including a miner named John Wallace who had seen both men in Allen's public house in Stobhill before ten on the night of the shootings, while both Innes and Vickers swore blind, they had spent the night in their beds. Helen Wilson was another valuable witness. She was outside her house at about ten on that Saturday night and saw a man near the field wall. At first, Helen believed it was her husband and shouted out to him, but on coming closer realised, it was her next-door neighbour, Vickers. She watched him walk into his house and as far as she was aware, he never left again. She did not hear his door open anyway. Innes also had a good witness, in a near neighbour called Mrs Walkinshaw. She thought she saw Innes come home about eleven at night. At about five on that Saturday morning, Mrs Walkinshaw was waking her daughters for their work and heard the crack of a shot from Innes' house.

The police may have hoped that the wound on Innes' jaw could have been incriminating, but instead, he had a good story. Innes claimed that, on the early morning of the 15th of December, a man named Andrew Bernard had come to his house to wake him, and while fumbling in the dark to answer the door, he had bumped into his shotgun, which fired and wounded him. That story confirmed Mrs Walkinshaw's memory of a shot in the early hours.

When the case came to the High Court, the witnesses spoke for Innes and Vickers, while the prosecution used the accounts of the gamekeepers. A majority of nine to six of the jury found them guilty, with the minority hoping for a not proven verdict. The judge, Lord Young, pronounced the death sentence. There was a public appeal against the executions, with well over a thousand signatures gathered, but the Home Secretary rejected it, despite the number of witnesses who claimed to have seen the two men elsewhere. Later, both Innes and Vickers confessed that they were indeed guilty of killing the gamekeepers. Vickers claimed that Innes had had a little too much to drink in the pub in Stobhill and had wanted to "have a shot." He also said he did not intend to kill Fortune but aimed at his legs; the angle of the hill deceived him, and he shot the keeper in the stomach. If these statements are correct, and there is no reason to doubt them as both men had already been found guilty, then the verdict was flawed: It was not a premeditated murder but the less serious crime of culpable homicide, which did not carry the death penalty.

It was not easy to hang somebody efficiently. Britain had a succession of official hangmen who travelled the length and breadth of the country performing judicial executions. Some of these men were well known, such as William Calcraft, who hanged an estimated 450 people; others did not achieve such fame. One of the latter was Bartholomew Binns, who had made such a complete mess of his last hanging that the condemned had taken eight hard minutes to die. The governors of Calton jail refused to hire such a man; they were not willing to prolong the agony of an already unhappy pair; instead, the authorities in Edinburgh advertised for a hangman. Of the two applications they received, that of James Berry seemed best. He was a former policeman from Bradford with no experience but a somewhat macabre interest in the subject. He had watched Calcraft's technique twice and had met another former executioner named William Marwood. The authorities chose Berry, and the Gorebridge poachers became his first customers.

The execution took place in Calton Jail on the 31st of March 1885. The jail rose grim and grey on the side of Calton Hill at the eastern entrance to Edinburgh, where Old St Andrews House now sits. The jail itself dated from 1817, a significant addition to Edinburgh's New Town, and replaced the terrible old Tolbooth, the Heart of Midlothian. The prominent site irritated many people, including the High Street Judge Lord Cockburn (of Cockburn Street fame) who said: "it has been a piece of undoubted bad taste to give so glorious an eminence to a prison." It was equally unpopular with the inmates, who thought it cold and impersonal with harsh discipline and mediocre food.

After the government outlawed public executions in the 1860s, Calton Jail became the site of Edinburgh's hangings. The governor had a scaffold built for the execution, carefully positioned so that the public could not watch; not even one of the five thousand people who climbed Calton Hill could see. Some of the hopeful spectators would be the usual ghouls that such occasions attracted, while many were friends and colleagues of the condemned who came to pay their last respects.

Some sources claim that Vickers was extremely penitent at the trouble he had caused his family but had hoped for a reprieve right to the moment that Berry pulled the white hood over his head. Then he fainted. When the governor ordered a black flag hoisted on the roof of the jail, the silent watchers on the hill knew that Innes and Vickers had poached their last pheasant. The two men were buried inside Calton jail, with quicklime thrown over their bodies. According to legend, a car park covers what little remains of both men.

The prison itself was demolished in the 1930s with the stones transferred to build the dam of the Hopes Reservoir in the Lammermuir Hills. The door of the condemned cell was retained and is now a feature of the Beehive Inn in Edinburgh's Grassmarket. Despite the lapse of time, people in Midlothian have not forgotten Innes and Vickers. And poaching? That will continue, under cover of night.

Chapter 18

TROUBLE AT VOGRIE

Visitors tend to admire the shattered remains of Scotland's medieval abbeys; Sir Walter Scott lauded them in prose and poetry, although locals treat them as part of the landscape with which they are long familiar. Yet, in their day, they were not only intrinsic to the spiritual life of the nation, but they were also economic forerunners, the pioneers of Scotland's wealth every bit as much as the mills and factories of the industrial revolution. While the Border abbeys were large-scale sheep farmers, the Cistercian foundation of Newbattle was at the forefront of lead and coal mining. From those monastic beginnings, coal mining became a staple industry in Midlothian.

Work down the pits was always dangerous, but sometimes the colliers themselves added to the hazards. In some mines of the nineteenth-century, pillars of coal were left between the floor and the roof. These "stoops" supported the roof, so when George Young and William Morrison hacked them away, rather than working at the hard-to-reach coal seam in the Engine Pit at Vogrie, in November 1855, their colleagues were not pleased. The police charged both men with reckless damage, but Sheriff Grahame only imposed a fine of ten shillings each as both men were very young.

However, not all the Coal Masters were ogres who drooled at the prospect of keeping their workers in constant toil and bondage. Some were humane and some who even wished to end the system of serfdom. One such was James Dewar of Vogrie. By the time the Dewars came to Vogrie in 1719, the house and estate were already ancient, but the Dewar family made the area their own. Vogrie lies between Gorebridge and Pathhead, looking toward Roman Camp Hill. The house lies within a swathe of parkland, with a ha-ha to keep any animals from straying and with the infant Tyne Water flowing brown and soft between beautiful woodland. The grounds are open to the public today, a peaceful lung and a lovely place for families to enjoy. In the nineteenth century, however, the Dewar family owned Vogrie as their private estate.

Nevertheless, even helping the colliers obtain a better life did not guarantee the Dewars of Vogrie immunity from the local criminals. It was on the 5th of May 1805 that somebody forced open the door to the servant's hall, crept through the house and stole some items of clothing that belonged to James Dewar, the son of the man who had helped the colliers. The thief lifted a green mixed coat, a pair of corduroy breeches and a hat. It was hardly a significant theft, as thefts go, but James Dewar was naturally displeased that somebody had robbed him. To some that may have seemed like a Robin Hood type crime, robbing the rich to give to the poor, but the thief did not just target Dewar but also stole from the servants. Six weeks after the theft of Dewar's clothes, there was another break-in, and this time the thief entered the room where Joseph Petty the groom was sleeping, used a pitchfork to force open his chest and removed some of his clothes. Not content with that he also stole from another groom named Charles Boyle; what he had not wanted he had thrown around the room, either in a rage or out of pure badness.

For a day or so, there was no clue as to whom the thief might be until a man on his way to visit the house found a small pile of clothes beneath the bridge over the River Tyne. At first, people thought that somebody had either committed suicide by throwing himself into the river, or had gone swimming and got into difficulties, but when there was no trace of a body, the authorities asked questions. When the staff at Vogrie House searched the clothes, they found the key to Dewar's small-beer cellar in one of the pockets. That made people wonder if the clothes may be related to the thefts, and there was conjecture that the thief might have stopped beside the river to change his clothes, putting on those he had stolen from Vogrie in exchange for the sadly battered garments left by the Tyne. Things became more interesting when one of the servants thought he recognised the clothes.

"They belonged to James Allan," he said.

Of course, once the servant mentioned the name, others also realised that James Allan was the man they sought. He was the perfect choice for the thief. At one time Allan had worked as a servant in Vogrie but, back in January, James Dewar had dismissed him. Allan had stomped away and joined the Royal Artillery – the Napoleonic War was at its height, and the army was always willing to accept recruits. However, Allan found that army life did not suit him any more than domestic service had, so he deserted and returned to his old stomping ground of Midlothian.

On the 27th of June, Petty and Boyle began a search for the man who had stolen their property. As they had worked with him, they had a pretty fair idea of Allan's haunts and headed for the change-house, the pub, at Ford, where James Pride the change-keeper listened to their story. Boyle had not been in the change-house long when he noticed a hat hanging on a peg by the door.

"Where did that hat come from?" He asked.

"James Allan sold it to me for fifteen shillings," Pride told him. "Three days since."

"It's the hat he stole from me," Boyle reclaimed his property. Now there was no doubt that Allan had been the thief.

From Ford, they walked to Haugh-head near Fala, another of Allan's drinking haunts. Frances Ales was the change-house keeper there and pointed out more clothes that Allan had sold. These belonged to Petty, but rather than burden himself with a bundle of clothes, he left them with Ales and followed the pub-trail to Blackshiels, only a few miles away on the main road south. That proved to be a good choice as Allan was already there.

However now they had caught up with him, Boyle and Petty seemed unsure what to do next. They sat and drank together for a while and then told him why they were here. As soon as he heard the reason, Allan bolted out of the door. Taken by surprise, Petty and Boyle chased in pursuit, only catching the thief when he staggered into a nearby field. This time they held Allan tightly, ordered a chaise and took him to Vogrie House, where he was securely locked away. There was no denying Allan's guilt as he was wearing Dewar's corduroy breeches, two of Petty's waistcoats, a pair of Boyle's worsted stockings, and had Dewar's hat jammed on his head. Even so, he claimed innocence until the authorities took him to Dalkeith and from there to jail in Edinburgh, where the sheriff questioned him.

Either the sheriff was very good at his job, or Allan was tired of evasion, for he admitted the robberies. He also said that the day after he robbed Petty and Boyle, he walked to Pride's change-house and then to Ales. Allan told Mrs Ales that he had argued with his brother, a millwright on Leith Walk and after a few days he would return to make peace with him. The stolen clothes were left there because he had not paid his bill, despite stealing £5 and some silver from Petty. He had hardly arrived in Blackshiels when Boyle and Petty found him.

Despite his admission, Allan pleaded not guilty when he appeared at the High Court. Perhaps he already guessed the inevitability of the sentence and hoped to delay things by a few hours. On the 22nd of July, he appeared before the Lord Advocate. With all the evidence before them, the jury had no hesitation in finding Allan guilty, and the judge sentenced him to hang. According to the press accounts, he "behaved in a very penitent and resigned manner" as Mr Porteous and the Reverent Thomas Macnight gave him spiritual guidance. He took his last breath in the Lawnmarket in Edinburgh, a tall, gentlemanly man of about 25, executed for a five-pound note and a few articles of clothing.

While Petty never saw his money again, he did get most of his clothing back. Most crimes were of such a petty nature, with a few items of clothing or a few pounds stolen, that one wonders why thieves risked their necks for such a paltry reward.

Chapter 19

PERILOUS PENICUIK

Penicuik is one of the most historic and vibrant towns in Midlothian. It occupies an enviable position on the west bank of the River North Esk and the flanks of the Pentland Hills. In 1770, Sir James Clerk expanded the original tiny hamlet with a planned village, and it grew in size, possibly because of its paper mills. Penicuik - the name means "hill of the cuckoos" - also has easy access to the capital and some delightful countryside. Penicuik also had its share of excitement, including a splendid riot in 1849.

It was common practice in old Scotland for gangs of labourers to come to the Lowlands at harvest time. These workers could be Highlanders or Irish, and they usually performed their work, took their pay and returned home with both sides happy with the bargain. However, there were occasions when drink-fuelled labourers caused pandemonium in small villages.

Such an event occurred in Penicuik on the night of Friday 28th September 1849. That was harvest time in Midlothian when the farmers kept one eye on the weather, one on the crops and both on the labourers they hired to get the latter in before the former turned wet. The harvesters used the old-fashioned, smooth-bladed sickle, often known as a scythe-hook, or a reaping-hook, which men swung at the full extent of their arm. In the eighteenth century, the Highland shearers had mostly been women, but after the Napoleonic wars, and the use of the scythe-hook rather than the smaller toothed sickle, Irishmen flooded into Scotland. As steamships replaced sail-powered vessels, the initial trickle of Irish became a flood with each harvest time attracting up to 40,000 seasonal workers.

On that Friday, the Irish shearers had been paid and hit the local pubs. As the saying goes, when the wine's in the wit is out, and the men soon began to quarrel amongst themselves. They came into Penicuik from the surrounding countryside and found more pubs, so after a while, what had started as a pleasant evening continued with more whisky, and the men became fighting-drunk.

When somebody notified the police, Constable James Mitchell marched along to calm the shearers down, with a handful of brave local men to back him up. The sight of an official uniform only made matters worse, and a shearer named Patrick Flynn slashed at Mitchell's head with his scythe-hook. Luckily Mitchell was sufficiently agile to lift his arm and parry, which resulted in a nasty wound on his forearm rather than across his throat. Reeling from the pain, Mitchell and the local men still managed to subdue Flynn while the other shearers fled. It was not until the next day that Superintendent List brought a body of reinforcements into Penicuik to hunt down the others and arrest them.

That was only one occasion when Irish labourers caused trouble for the Penicuik police. In November 1850, it was men working at Edinburgh's new water supply at Crawley Springs near the Bush who were the problem. It was the first Saturday of the month, payday, and the labourers headed to a pub at Newmilton, north of Auchendinny. The local policeman, Constable McFarlane knew he was vastly outnumbered so asked for help, and Constable Mitchell came to back him up. Mitchell already had experience of drunken Irishmen, so would be wary of any possible trouble.

About eleven that night Mrs Buchan, who kept a lodging house in one of the two dozen or so cottages in Newmilton, complained to the constables that an Irishman named Campbell had smashed one of her windows and had been hammering at her front door. Both constables approached Campbell, who denied any wrongdoing and resisted as

McFarlane arrested him. McFarlane's house doubled as a police office, so they wrestled Campbell in that direction until a mob of Irishmen erupted from the pub and attacked them to free their colleague.

The Irish picked on McFarlane first, jumping in from him from behind, knocking him to the ground and kicking him as he sprawled there. Mitchell turned to help, and an Irishman immediately felled him, while Campbell escaped, as the rest of the Irish scooped him up and fled. When they got back to their feet, Mitchell had six distinct wounds and McFarlane three.

Such events did not seem unusual in Penicuik. On Saturday 26th January 1856, the two teenaged Matheson brothers were standing at a corner of Penicuik High Street when a bunch of Irish drainers attacked them. Taken by surprise, the brothers could not defend themselves; one had his leg broken and the other his head split. As they lay on the ground and the Irish put the boot in, a scattering of young Penicuik men tried to help. However, more Irish appeared, outnumbering the locals and more used to violence. They used weapons such as stones and broken fences, and when the dust cleared, there were eight injured Penicuik youths.

As so often, the local police were outnumbered, so asked for reinforcements. Early on the Sunday morning, Chief Constable List brought in a body of uniformed constables, and they scoured the streets for any Irishmen who looked to have been involved. The police arrested five Irishmen and sent them off to Calton jail in Edinburgh.

There were other such incidents, but to repeat them would become tedious. Sufficient to say that rural life in nineteenth-century Penicuik was never dull with always the possibility of sudden violence breaking out. Ah, the good old days!

EPILOGUE

In a book of this size, it is possible to include only a fraction of the episodes, crimes and so-called-crimes that occurred in Midlothian during the eighteenth and nineteenth centuries. The story of the Midlothian miners alone deserves at least a full volume to do the subject justice. The story of the Midlothian police and its work deserves another, while the story of the military, with its Midlothian connections and all the campaigns and drama, would easily fill a third.

The conditions under which the colliers lived and worked are nearly unbelievable, especially when compared to the lifestyles of the landowners who profited from their labour. However, most ordinary people faced hardship in the eighteenth and nineteenth centuries, as a brief look at the lives of soldiers, fishermen, factory hands, or farm labourers will ascertain. The army too has altered, although the danger of overseas postings remains as real as ever. And crime continues. In the nineteenth century, Midlothian crime was mainly petty, silly drink-fuelled assaults or small acts of theft, but to the people involved, they would be important. When a few pennies was all the difference between poverty and relative comfort, the theft of a week's wage was a major calamity.

Today Midlothian is changing again. The mines are all closed, and the towns are expanding as they take on new roles as part of Edinburgh's commuter belt. The countryside remains, although slowly being eroded, and the hills, although pressure from a growing population is slowly and steadily eating away at the once-secluded areas. New roads slice through, and aircraft roar over to land at Turnhouse, but always Midlothian remains, God's own country, as a Dalkeith policeman once told me, and I cannot argue with that.

Malcolm Archibald.

ABOUT THE AUTHOR

Born and raised in Edinburgh, Malcolm Archibald has Midlothian roots that extend to at least the eighteenth century. Married to a local girl in Newtongrange, he was educated at the University of Dundee. He has experience in many fields and writes about the Scottish whaling industry as well as historical fiction and fantasy.

SELECTED BIBLIOGRAPHY

Archibald, Malcolm, (2016), *Dance if ye Can: A Dictionary of Scottish Battles*, (Creativia, Helsinki)

Arnot, R. Page, (1955), *A History of the Scottish Miners*, George Allen & Unwin Ltd, London.

Barrie, David (2008), *Police in the Age of Improvement: Police Development and the Civic Tradition in Scotland*, 1775 – 1865, Devon: Willan Publishing.

Burt, Edmond, (1754, 1998), *Burt's Letters from the North of Scotland*, Edinburgh: Birlinn. Cameron, David Kerr (1978), The Ballad and the Plough, London: Victor Gollancz.

Cameron, Joy (1983), *Prisons and Punishment in Scotland from the Middle Ages to the Present,* Edinburgh: Canongate.

Chesney, Kellow (1970), *The Victorian Underworld*, London: Maurice Temple Smith Ltd.

Cobbett, William, (1830, 2001) *Rural Rides*, London, Penguin.

Cockburn, Lord (1888, 1983), *Circuit Journeys*, Edinburgh: David Douglas; Hawick: Byway Books.

Cockburn, Lord (1856), *Memorials of his Time*, Edinburgh.

Donnelly, Daniel and Scott, Kenneth (editors) (2005), *Policing Scotland*, Devon: Willan Publishing.

Fenton, Alexander, (1987), *Country Life in Scotland: Our Rural Past*, Edinburgh: John Donald.

Godfrey, Barry and Lawrence, Paul (2005), *Crime and Justice 1750-1950*, Devon: Willan Publishing

Grant, Elizabeth, (1911), *Memoirs of a Highland Lady*, Edinburgh: John Murray.
Holmes, Richard, (2001), *Redcoat*, London: HarperCollins
Haswell, Jock, (1975), *The British Army*, London, BCA.
Jones, David, (1982), *Crime, Protest, Community and Police in Nineteenth Century Britain*, London: Routledge & Kegan Paul.
Knepper, Paul, (2007), *Criminology and Social Policy*, London: Sage Publications.
McLaren, Duncan (1858), *The Rise and Progress of Whisky Drinking in Scotland and the Working of the Public Houses (Scotland) Act, commonly called the Forbes McKenzie Act*, Glasgow; Edinburgh: Scottish Temperance League.
Smith, Gavin D. (2002), *The Secret Still: Scotland's Clandestine Whisky Makers*, Edinburgh: Birlinn.
Smout, T. C. (1969), *A History of the Scottish People, 1560-1830*, London: Collins.
Smout, T. C. (1987), *A Century of the Scottish People, 1830-1950*, London: Collins.
Stevenson, Robert, (1819) *Report relative to various lines of railway, from the coal-field of Mid-Lothian to the City of Edinburgh and Port of Leith: With plans and sections.*
Wilson, John James, (2012), *The Annals of Penicuik: Being a History of the Parish and of the Village*, Classic Reprint.
Midlothian Council Archives: The Black Collection GB 584 BLA: BLA 1; BLA 2

Newspapers:

Caledonian Mercury
Newcastle Courant
Scots Magazine

Dear reader,

We hope you enjoyed reading *Midlothian Mayhem*. Please take a moment to leave a review, even if it's a short one. Your opinion is important to us.

Discover more books by Malcolm Archibald at https://www.nextchapter.pub/authors/malcolm-archibald

Want to know when one of our books is free or discounted? Join the newsletter at http://eepurl.com/bqqB3H

Best regards,

Malcolm Archibald and the Next Chapter Team

You could also like:

Strange Tales of Scotland by Jack Strange

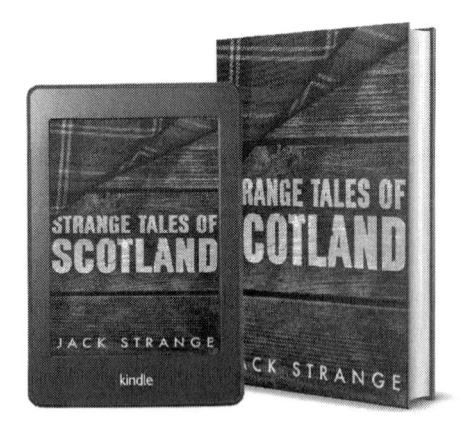

To read the first chapter for free, please head to:
https://www.nextchapter.pub/books/strange-tales-of-scotland-scottish-mysteries

Printed in Great Britain
by Amazon